MW00527798

GEMINI
WITCH

♊

©JAMES C. WELCH

Ivo Dominguez, Jr. (Georgetown, DE) has been active in the magickal community since 1978. He is one of the founders of Keepers of the Holly Chalice, the first Assembly of the Sacred Wheel coven. He currently serves as one of the Elders in the Assembly. Ivo is the author of several books, including *The Four Elements of the Wise* and *Practical Astrology for Witches and Pagans*. In his mundane life, he has been a computer programmer, the executive director of an AIDS/HIV service organization, a bookstore owner, and many other things. Visit him at www.ivodominguezjr.com.

© CARRIE MEYER

Laura Tempest Zakroff is a professional artist, author, and Modern Traditional Witch based in New England. She holds a BFA from The Rhode Island School of Design and her artwork has received awards and honors worldwide. Her work embodies myth and the esoteric through her drawings and paintings, jewelry, talismans, and other designs. Laura is the author of several best-selling titles from Llewellyn including *Weave the Liminal*, *Sigil Witchery*, and *Anatomy of a Witch*, as well as the artist/author of *The Liminal Spirits Oracle* and *The Anatomy of a Witch Oracle*. Laura edited *The New Aradia: A Witch's Handbook to Magical Resistance* and *The Gorgon's Guide to Magical Resistance* from Revelore Press. She is the creative force behind several community events and teaches workshops worldwide. Visit her at http://www.lauratempestzakroff.com.

UNLOCK THE MAGIC OF YOUR SUN SIGN

GEMINI WITCH

Ⅱ

IVO DOMINGUEZ, JR.
LAURA TEMPEST ZAKROFF

Llewellyn Publications
Woodbury, Minnesota

FIRST EDITION
First Printing, 2023

Art direction and cover design by Shira Atakpu
Book design by Christine Ha
Interior art by the Llewellyn Art Department
Sigil (page 208) by Laura Tempest Zakroff
Tarot Original 1909 Deck © 2021 with art created by Pamela Colman Smith and Arthur Edward Waite. Used with permission of LoScarabeo.
The Gemini Correspondences appendix is excerpted with permission from *Llewellyn's Complete Book of Correspondences: A Comprehensive & Cross-Referenced Resource for Pagans & Wiccans* © 2013 by Sandra Kynes.

Llewellyn Publications is a registered trademark of Llewellyn Worldwide Ltd.

Library of Congress Cataloging-in-Publication Data (Pending)
ISBN: 978-0-7387-7282-0

Llewellyn Worldwide Ltd. does not participate in, endorse, or have any authority or responsibility concerning private business transactions between our authors and the public.

All mail addressed to the author is forwarded but the publisher cannot, unless specifically instructed by the author, give out an address or phone number.

Any internet references contained in this work are current at publication time, but the publisher cannot guarantee that a specific location will continue to be maintained. Please refer to the publisher's website for links to authors' websites and other sources.

Llewellyn Publications
A Division of Llewellyn Worldwide Ltd.
2143 Wooddale Drive
Woodbury, MN 55125-2989
www.llewellyn.com

Printed in the United States of America

Other Books by Ivo Dominguez, Jr.

The Four Elements of the Wise
Keys to Perception: A Practical Guide to Psychic Development
Practical Astrology for Witches and Pagans
Casting Sacred Space
Spirit Speak

Other Books by Laura Tempest Zakroff

Sigil Witchery
Visual Alchemy
Weave the Liminal
Anatomy of a Witch
The Liminal Spirits Oracle
Anatomy of a Witch Oracle
The Witch's Cauldron
The Witch's Altar (with Jason Mankey)

Other Books in The Witch's Sun Sign Series

Aries Witch
Taurus Witch
Cancer Witch
Leo Witch
Virgo Witch
Libra Witch
Scorpio Witch
Sagittarius Witch
Capricorn Witch
Aquarius Witch
Pisces Witch

CONTENTS

* Contents *

SPELLS, RECIPES, AND PRACTICES

Ivo Dominguez, Jr.

This is the third book in the Witch's Sun Sign series. There are twelve volumes in this series with a book for every Sun sign, but with a special focus on witchcraft. This series explores and honors the gifts, perspectives, and joys of being a witch through the perspective of their Sun sign. Each book has information on how your sign affects your magick and life experiences with insights provided by witches of your Sun sign, as well as spells, rituals, and practices to enrich your witchcraft. This series is geared toward helping witches grow, develop, and integrate the power of their Sun sign into all their practices. Each book in the series has ten writers, so there are many takes on the meaning of being a witch of a particular sign. All the books in the Witch's Sun Sign series are a sampler of possibilities, with pieces that are deep, fun, practical, healing, instructive, revealing, and authentic.

Welcome to the Gemini Witch

I'm Ivo Dominguez, Jr., and I've been a witch and an astrologer for over forty years. In this book, and in the whole series, I've written the chapters focused on astrological information and collaborated with the other writers. For the sake of transparency, I am a Sagittarius, and most of the nine other writers for this book are Gemini.[1] The chapters focused on the lived experience of being a Gemini witch were written by my coauthor, Laura Tempest Zakroff, who is a visionary artist, author, dancer, designer, and community organizer and has been a Modern Traditional Witch for more than two decades. The spells and shorter pieces written for this book come from a diverse group of strong Gemini witches. Their practices will give you a deeper understanding of yourself as a Gemini and as a witch. With the information, insights, and methods offered here, your Gemini nature and your witchcraft will be better united. The work of becoming fully yourself entails finding, refining, and merging all the parts that make your life and identity. This all sounds very serious, but the content of this book will run from lighthearted to profound to do justice to the topic. Moreover, this book has practical suggestions on using the power of your Sun sign to improve your craft as a witch. There are many books on

---

1. The exceptions are Dawn Aurora Hunt, who contributes a recipe for each sign in the series, and Sandra Kynes, whose correspondences are listed in the appendix.

Gemini or astrology or witchcraft; this book is about whole-heartedly being a Gemini witch.

There is a vast amount of material available in books, blogs, memes, and videos targeted at Gemini. The content presented in these ranges from serious to snarky, and a fair amount of it is less than accurate or useful. After reading this book, you will be better equipped to tell which of these you can take to heart and use, and which are fine for a laugh but not much more. There is a good chance you will be flipping back to reread some chapters to get a better understanding of some of the points being made. This book is meant to be read more than once, and some parts of it may become reference material you will use for years. Consider keeping a folder, digital or paper, for your notes and ideas on being a Gemini witch.

What You Will Need

Knowing your Sun sign is enough to get quite a bit out of this book. However, to use all the material in this book, you will need your birth chart to verify your Moon sign and rising sign. In addition to your birth date, you will need the location and the time of your birth as exactly as possible. If you don't know your birth time, try to get a copy of your birth certificate (though not all birth certificates list times). If it is reasonable and you feel comfortable, you can ask family members for information. They may remember an exact time, but even narrowing it down to a range of hours will be useful. There is a solution to not having your exact birth time. Since it takes moments to create birth charts using software, you can run birth charts that are thirty minutes apart over the span of hours that contains your possible birth times. By reading the chapters that describe the characteristics of Moon signs and rising signs, you can reduce the pile of possible charts to a few contenders. Read the descriptions and find the chart whose combination of Moon sign and rising sign rings true to you. There are more refined techniques a professional astrologer can use to get closer to a chart that is more accurate. However, knowing your Sun sign, Moon sign, and rising sign is all you need for this book. There are numerous websites that offer free basic birth charts you can view online. For a fee, more detailed charts are available on these sites.

You may want to have an astrological wall calendar or an astrological day planner to keep track of the sign and phase of the Moon. You will want to keep track of what your ruling planet, Mercury, is doing. Over time as your knowledge grows, you'll probably start looking at where all the planets are, what aspects they are making, and when they are retrograde or direct. You could do this all on an app or a website, but it is often easier to flip through a calendar or planner to see what is going on. Flipping forward and back through the weeks and months ahead can give you a better sense of how to prepare for upcoming celestial influences. Moreover, the calendars and planner contain basic background information about astrology and are a great start for studying astrology.

You're a Gemini and So Much More

Every person is unique, complex, and a mixture of traits that can clash, complement, compete, or collaborate with each other. This book focuses on your Gemini Sun sign and provides starting points for understanding your Moon sign and rising sign. It cannot answer all your questions or be a perfect fit because of all the other parts that make you an individual. However, you will find more than enough to enrich and deepen your witchcraft as a Gemini. There will also be descriptions you won't agree with or you think do not portray you. In some instances, you will be correct, and in other cases, you may come around to acknowledging that the information does apply to you. Astrology can be used for magick, divination, personal development, and more. No matter the purpose, your understanding of astrology will change over time as your life unfolds and your experience and self-knowledge broaden. You will probably return to this book several times as you find opportunities to use more of the insights and methods.

5

This may seem like strange advice to find in a book for the Gemini witch, but remember that you are more than a Gemini witch. In the process of claiming the identity of being a witch, it is common to want to have a clear and firm definition of who you are. Sometimes this means overidentifying with a category, such as fire witch, herb witch, crystal witch, kitchen witch, and so on. It is useful to become aware of the affinities you have so long as you do not limit and bind yourself to being less than you are. The best use for this book is to uncover all the Gemini parts of you so you can integrate them well. The finest witches I know have well-developed specialties but also are well rounded in their knowledge and practices.

Onward!

With all that said, the Sun is the starting point for your power and your journey as a witch. The first chapter is about the profound influence your Sun sign has, so don't skip through the table of contents; please start at the beginning. After that, Laura will dive into magick and practices that come naturally to Gemini witches. I'll be walking you through the benefits of picking the right times, places, and things to energize your Gemini magick. Laura will also share a couple of real-life personal stories on how to manage the busy lives that Geminis choose, as well as advice on the best ways to protect yourself spiritually and set good boundaries when you really need to. I'll introduce you to how your Moon sign and your rising sign shape your witchcraft. Laura offers great stories about how her Gemini nature comes forward in her life as a witch, and then gives suggestions on self-care and self-awareness. I'll share a full ritual with you to call on the spirit of your sign. Lastly, Laura offers her wisdom on how to become a better Gemini witch. Throughout the whole book, you'll find tables of correspondences, spells, recipes, practices, and other treasures to add to your practices.

HOW YOUR SUN POWERS YOUR MAGICK

Ivo Dominguez, Jr.

The first bit of astrology people generally learn is their Sun sign. Some enthusiastically embrace the meaning of their Sun sign and apply it to everything in their life. They feel their Sun is shining and all is well in the world. Then at some point, they'll encounter someone who will, with a bit of disdain, enlighten them on the limits of Sun sign astrology. They feel their Sun isn't enough, and they scramble to catch up. What comes next is usually the discovery that they have a Moon sign, a rising sign, and all the rest of the planets in an assortment of signs. Making sense of all this additional information is daunting as it requires quite a bit of learning and/or an astrologer to guide you through the process. Wherever you are on this journey into the world of astrology, at some point you will circle back around and rediscover that the Sun is still in the center.

The Sun in your birth chart shows where life and spirit came into the world to form you. It is the keeper of your spark of spirit and the wellspring of your power. Your Sun is in Gemini, so that is the flavor, the color, the type of energy that is at your core. You are your whole birth chart, but it is your Gemini Sun that provides the vital force that moves throughout all parts of your life. When you work in harmony and alignment with your Sun, you have access to more life and the capacity to live it better. This is true for all people, but this advice takes on a special meaning for those who are witches. The root of a witch's magick power is revealed by their Sun sign. You can draw on many kinds of energy, but the type of energy you attract with greatest ease is Gemini. The more awareness and intention you apply to connecting with and acting as a conduit for that Gemini Sun, the more effective you will be as a witch.

The more you learn about the meaning of a Gemini Sun, the easier it will be to find ways to make that connection. To be effective in magick, divination, and other categories of workings, it is vital to understand yourself—your motivations, drives, attractions, etc.—so you can refine your intentions, questions, and desired outcomes. Understanding your Sun sign is an important step in that process. One of the goals shared by both witchcraft and astrology is to affirm and to integrate the totality of your nature to live your best life. The glyph for the Sun in astrology is a dot with a circle around it. Your Gemini Sun is the dot and the circle, your center, and your circumference. It is your beginning and your journey. It is also the core of your personal Wheel of the Year, the seasons of your life that repeat, have resonances, but are never the same.

How Gemini Are You?

The Sun is the hub around which the planets circle. Its gravity pulls the planets to keep them in their courses and bends space-time to create the place we call our solar system. The Sun in your birth chart tugs on every other part of your chart in a similar way. Everything is both bound and free, affected but seeking its own direction. When people encounter descriptions of Gemini traits, they will often begin to make a list of which things apply to them and which don't. Some will say they are the epitome of Gemini traits, others will claim that they are barely Gemini, and many will be somewhere in between. Evaluating how closely or not you align with the traditional characteristics of a Gemini is not a particularly useful approach to understanding your sign. If you are a Gemini, you have all the Gemini traits somewhere within you. What varies from person to person is the expression of those traits. Some traits express fully in a classic form, others are blocked from expressing or are modified, and sometimes there is a reaction to behave as the opposite of what is expected. As a Gemini, and especially as a witch, you have the capacity to activate dormant traits, to shape functioning traits, and to tone down overactive traits.

The characteristics and traits of signs are tendencies, drives, and affinities. Gravity encourages a ball to roll down a hill. A plant's leaves will grow in the direction of sunlight. The warmth of a fire will draw people together on a cold night. A flavor you enjoy will entice you to take another bite of your food. Your Gemini Sun urges you to be and to act like a Gemini. That said, you also have free will and volition to make other choices. Moreover, the rest of your birth chart and the ever-changing celestial influences are also shaping your options, moods, and drives. The more you become aware of the traits and behaviors that come with being a Gemini, the easier it will be to choose how you express them. Most people want to have the freedom to make their own choices, but for a Gemini, it is essential.

As a witch, you have additional tools to work with the Gemini energy. You can choose when to access and how you shape the qualities of Gemini as they come forth in your life. You can summon the energy of Gemini, name the traits you desire, and manifest them. You can also banish or neutralize or ground what you don't need. You can find where your Gemini energy short-circuits, where it glitches, and unblock it. You can examine your uncomfortable feelings and your less-than-perfect behaviors to seek the shadowed places within so you can heal or integrate them. Gemini is also a spirit and a current of collective consciousness that is vast in size—a group mind and archetype. Gemini is not limited to humanity; it engages with plants, animals, minerals, and all the physical and nonphysical beings of the Earth and all its associated realms. As a witch, you can call upon and work with the spiritual entity that is Gemini. You can live your life as a ritual. The motion of your life can be a dance to the tune and rhythm of the heavens.

The Gemini Glyph

The glyph for Gemini looks like the Roman numeral for the number two, though sometimes the lines are curved rather than straight. It is more than a reference to the twins who are the symbol for this sign.

The vertical lines reaching upward and downward that connect with the horizontal lines express a dialogue between the lower and higher planes. This linkage can be seen as spanning your personal consciousness from the depths to the heights. The glyph also can be seen as a doorway or a portal—the portal through which you see the world and perceive it. This is the opening through which your wide and fast consciousness must be narrowed into words that fit. It also reminds you that all you see, hear, and perceive must pass through this narrow gate. No wonder you are always shifting the angle to let more in. The parallel lines are like mirror reflections of each other, suggesting that you see the world as you see yourself. As your self-understanding grows, your reflection of the outer world into your inner world is truer. The glyphs for all the air signs have parallel lines.

Use your imagination to see this glyph as a representation of how you are a sibling to everything that exists. You have a relationship with all you observe. The symmetry of the glyph also suggests the capacity to find analogies between all things. This is the symbol of a translator, an interpreter, and a channel for communication. It is also the pylon gate to the inner temple that sits between the mortal and immortal realms. This is where your magick enters and exits the world.

By meditating on the glyph, you will develop a deeper understanding of what it is to be a Gemini. You may also come up with your own personal gnosis or story about the glyph that can be a key that is uniquely yours. The glyph for Gemini can be used in a similar fashion to the scribing of an invoking pentacle that is used to open the gates to the elemental realms. However, instead of the elemental realms, this glyph opens the way to the realm of mind and spirit that is the source of Gemini. To make this glyph work, you need to deeply ingrain the feeling of scribing this glyph. Visually, it is a simple glyph, so memorizing it is easy, but having a kinesthetic feel for it turns it into magick. Spend some time doodling the glyph on paper. Try drawing the glyph on your palm with a finger for several repetitions as that adds several layers of sensation and memory patterns.

Whenever you need access to more of your magickal energy, scribe the Gemini glyph in your mind, on your hand, in the air—however you can. Then pull and channel and feel your center fill with whatever you need. It takes very little time to open this connection using the glyph. Consider making this one of the practices you use to get ready to do divination, spell work, ritual, or just to start your day.

Gemini Patterns

This is a short list of patterns, guidelines, and predilections for Gemini Sun people to get you started. If you keep a book of shadows, or a journal, or files on a digital device to record your thoughts and insights on magickal work, you may wish to create your own list to expand upon these. The process of observing, summarizing, and writing down your own ideas in a list is a great way to learn about your sign.

- Geminis always question their perceptions, their culture, and all the people around them.

- You zip about collecting data and impressions until suddenly your thoughts and beliefs become a crisp and detailed image.

- You are sometimes accused of not paying attention. Instead, you are paying attention to so many things at once that others may not follow your chain of thought.

- Reality is flexible for you because you keep discovering alternate meanings and perspectives. This applies equally to objects, abstractions, people, and so on.

- Geminis readily shift into a more open and non-judgmental frame of mind and communicate with people who are very different from themselves.

- When you are in a good mood, it radiates to people around you. Your smiles and laughter move through a room like a gentle breeze.

- You can sabotage yourself by thinking of all the many ways your choices can go wrong. This can lock you up, which is the worst place for a Gemini.

- When you are under deadlines or other kinds of pressure, you become restless and scattered. Break things up into smaller steps and chunks and you'll do better.

- You love mental stimulation, spontaneous escapades, and witty conversations. These recharge your soul.

◎ Until you reach the end of your endurance, you are awfully good at hiding distress. Let your friends know if you need hugs, space, hot tea, or whatever you need to be reassured.

◎ Periodically, you need to do a hard reboot on your life. When that happens, look at the world as if you were a child seeing it for the first time.

◎ Geminis can spend too much time in their head. Your ruling planet Mercury also rules arts and crafts, so doing things with your hands is a great way to express yourself and relax.

◎ You enjoy books, movies, games, music, and pretty much any kind of media. Don't feel guilty about the time spent with these activities. It is not a waste of time if you are enjoying yourself.

◎ Being a Gemini does not mean you don't need alone time. You need alone time to process and make sense of all your experiences.

○ Stereotypically, the sign of the twins is said to be two personalities in one body. It is much more than that. It is the dialogue between you and your higher Self, you and your lower Self, you and your ancestors, and so on.

○ Sometimes in your excitement to share information, you may cross the line into sharing what you shouldn't. Listen to yourself as you speak; things can't be unsaid.

○ You are versatile, curious, quick moving, and adaptable. These are great traits that can be misunderstood, and people may say things that hurt your feelings. Focus on what caused the misunderstanding and it won't be as bothersome.

○ Part of your work in the world is to surprise people. Sometimes you are a trickster, other times a teacher, or perhaps a priestx, and in all cases you break people out of dull routines.

◎ When you commit to a person, a project, or an ideal, you go all in. The reason some say Geminis are fickle or won't commit is because they aren't aware of the long mental journey you take to make your choices.

◎ You have a quick mind, but the nuts and bolts of your finances and business matters do not excite you. Either find a way to make these more interesting or get someone else to do it for you.

Mutable Air

The four elements come in sets of three that repeat. The modalities known as cardinal, fixed, and mutable are three different flavors or styles of manifestation for the elements. The twelvefold pattern that is the backbone of astrology comes from the twelve combinations produced from four elements times three modalities. As you go around the wheel of the zodiac,  the order of the elements is always fire, earth, air, then water, while the modalities are always in the order of cardinal, fixed, then mutable. Each season begins in the cardinal modality, reaches its peak in the fixed modality, and transforms to the next season in the mutable modality. The cardinal modality is the energy of creation bursting forth, coming into being, and spreading throughout the world. The fixed modality is the harmonization of energy so that it becomes and remains fully itself and is preserved. Fixed does not mean static or passive; it is the work of maintaining creation. The mutable modality is the energy of flux that is flexibility, transformation, death, and rebirth.

Gemini is the third sign in the zodiac, so it is air of the mutable modality. This is why a Gemini witch can call upon deep reserves of mental energy and the ability to find meaningful connections. Although as a Gemini witch you can call upon air in all its forms, it is easiest to draw upon mutable air.

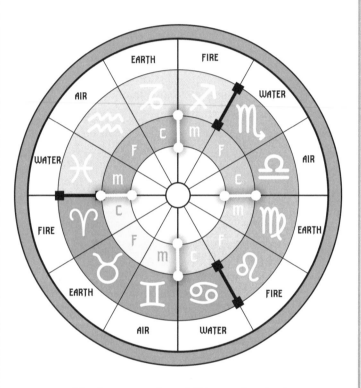

The elements and modalities on the wheel

Mercury, Your Ruling Planet

Your Sun sign determines the source and the type of energy you have in your core. The ruling planet for a sign reveals your go-to moves and your intuitive or habitual responses for expressing that energy. Your ruling planet provides a curated set of prebuilt responses and custom-tailored stances for you to use in day-to-day life. Mercury is the ruling planet for Gemini. This may bring to mind the Greek Hermes or the Roman Mercury, the fleetfooted messengers of their pantheons. However, the planet Mercury and how it influences Gemini is more complicated than being a messenger for divine beings. Mercury is the whole process of the mind from perception to thought, communication, and contemplation. Mercury is also the power to travel through different layers of reality. Mercury is the herald and psychopomp who is allowed to go everywhere. Mercury is the root of all curiosity. This in turn gives a strong desire to explore as much as possible. The influence of Mercury makes Gemini seek joy through the accumulation of life experiences and the review and reworking of all they've seen.

Gemini witches are more strongly affected by whatever Mercury is doing in the heavens. It is useful to keep track of the aspects that Mercury is making with other planets. You can get basic information on what aspects mean and when they are happening in astrological calendars and online resources. You will feel Mercury retrogrades more strongly than most people, but you can find ways to make them useful periods to analyze what you've already done. Gemini witches will notice that the impact of the Mercury retrograde will start earlier and end a few days later than the listed duration. Also, when Mercury in the heavens is in Gemini, you will feel an extra boost of energy. The first step to using the power of Mercury is to pay attention to what it is doing, how you feel, and what is happening in your life.

Witches have the gift to shift their relationship with the powers they work with and the powers that influence them. As a Gemini witch, you are connected to the power of Mercury. By paying close attention to how those energies affect you, it becomes possible to harness those energies to purposes you choose. Mercury can be as great a source of energy for a Gemini witch as the element of air. Although there is some overlap between the qualities and capacities assigned to Mercury and air, the differences are greater. Mercury shapes how you form thoughts and words out of the stream of consciousness. Air is the medium that forms consciousness and sensory information. Mercury has the power to motivate or block your actions and to separate or join heart and mind. Air connects the minds and spirits of all beings. Mercury is all symbolic exchanges, not just communication. Mercury is commerce, sacred offerings, and the principle of reciprocity. Air is the principle of agency, of interconnectedness, and composure. Over time, you can map out the overlapping regions and the differences between Mercury and air. Using both planetary and elemental resources can give you a much broader range and more finesse.

Gemini and the Zodiacal Wheel

The order of the signs in the zodiac can also be seen as a creation story where the run of the elements repeats three times. Gemini is in the first third of the zodiac, which is the first appearance of the four elements in the story of the universe. They are fresh from the maelstrom of creation; they are closest to the source. Gemini remembers the moment of creation. The air of Gemini is the most primal of all the versions of the element of air.

Although true for all witches, the Gemini witch needs to apply themselves to discovering how to perceive and communicate with spiritual forces and make them understandable in the physical world. When you can regularly connect with being a speaker and a conduit for your magick, the people and projects that matter to you will flourish. This is the full expression of being in the first quarter of the zodiac. You can make progress in this quest through meditation and inner journeys, but that alone will not do. The Gemini witch learns by doing, seeing, touching, questioning, learning, and repeating the process. Although Geminis are sometimes stereotyped as ungrounded or preoccupied, it is more accurate to say that they are trying to think as widely and as deeply as possible. When a Gemini witch connects to the spiritual qualities of their air, they become a teacher and a voice for the magick of the world.

The sign and planet rulers on zodiac wheel

GEMINI
CORRESPONDENCES

♊

Power: To Think

Keyword: Versatility

Roles: Messenger, Shape-Shifter

Ruling Planet: Mercury ☿

Element: Mutable Air

Colors: Light Yellow and Orange

Shape: Octagon

Metals: Mercury, but for practical reasons,
Aluminum or Platnium

Body Part Ruled: Shoulders and Upper Arms

Day of the Week: Wednesday

Affirmation:
*When I let curiousity and purpose
guide my seeking, joy follows.*

WITCHCRAFT THAT COMES NATURALLY TO A GEMINI

Laura Tempest Zakroff

In this section, we'll explore some of the magick and practices that come naturally to Gemini witches. I may be a bit biased, but I think we tend to be an exceptionally magickal and creative collection of folks. We like to experiment, push boundaries, ask lots of questions, and explore the unexpected. We follow the beat of our drum, which makes some people uncomfortable but excites and inspires others. All of these things make a great recipe for magickal living.

One of the strongest abilities inherently present in Geminis is the ability to perceive multiple aspects at once. We rarely dismiss anything as being simply black or white, but rather are tuned in to many levels of nuance and possibilities. We often have a hard time labeling kinds of magick as positive or negative, good or bad, baneful or blessed because we clue in to the numerous factors and dynamics at play. Others may ask us, "Is this dark or light?" and it's not uncommon for us to answer, "Both!" For example, we know a healing spell can be harmful if misapplied, a hex can bring justice and peace, and protection spells can accidentally hide people or things. Every working or action not only has a reaction, but rather reactions—and we can spend a lot of time considering those to the point of overthinking. But in the end, when we follow our intuition, we can work some seriously powerful magick.

Our ability to decipher multiple aspects of a given situation and our graceful way with words help us be exceptionally adept at conflict resolution and redirection. As we're able to understand both sides of a situation, we're very good at defusing tempers, helping folks meet in the middle to dissolve arguments, and otherwise being harbingers of calm to potential hot spots.

Geminis also have a knack for humor and wordplay that can surprise folks, drastically shifting the energy of a tense moment into something more conducive for all. You may have heard the expression "laughter is powerful medicine," and we know how to work it well! Others may dismiss us for not taking matters seriously enough, but we're actually tapping into the archetype of the divine trickster. Found in myth and folklore from all over the globe, the divine trickster is someone who is exceptionally smart or wise and uses that knowledge to defy convention, bend the rules, and disrupt the status quo. As Gemini is ruled by Mercury, it shouldn't be surprising that Hermes is known to be a trickster. Other divine tricksters from around the world include Coyote, Anansi, Loki, Br'er Rabbit, Puck, Papa Legba, Set, and Māui. While they tend to get a bad rap as troublemakers, many of them are deeply connected to or considered responsible for human civilization. Their alternative or unique viewpoints cause society to examine itself, often stimulating growth and creativity.

Deities and Spirits

Beyond a tendency to embody the divine trickster at times, you might wonder how else Geminis relate to deities and spirits. Due to the twin nature of our sign, Gemini witches naturally have a knack for embracing dualities and multitudes. This means we rarely have trouble embracing ideas centered around gods and spirits. We're already having a conversation with ourselves, so it's easy to loop in a few more. We tend to be animists and polytheistic in nature as well, though not typically devotional in practice or exclusive in who we connect with or how. We are often drawn to deities who have interesting histories and multiple interpretations, as well as those who specialize in learning and communication. At the same time, we'll talk to pretty much anything and everything, including inanimate objects.

In the following section, you'll find deities Gemini witches often connect with. Keep in mind that your relationship with deity or spirit is exactly that—your own. There's nothing wrong if your favorite deity isn't on the list below. The list is simply a sampling of some popular ones. If any intrigue you, I recommend doing more research and finding out more about them.

A Selection of Deities Who Embody Aspects of Gemini:

+ Athena—The patron deity of Athens, Greece, Gemini witches can appreciate the multitude of intellectual aspects Athena represents. Born out of Zeus's forehead, she embodies wisdom, inspiration, creativity, weaving, mathematics, strategy, and strength. She is also a goddess of war and protection, often accompanied by an owl.

+ Hekate (or Hecate)—Often depicted as a three-fold figure in Greek sculpture holding torches, keys, and serpents, Hekate is known to be a goddess of the crossroads, associated with witchcraft, magick, and the underworld. We find duality in that she is a bringer of illumination but also navigates through darkness and death.

+ Hermes (Greek)/Mercury (Roman)—Hermes is a messenger of the gods, often depicted with winged sandals and the caduceus (staff with two intwined serpents). He is able to easily move between the heavens, Earth, and underworlds. As a herald, he's linked with communication, and his mobility between the worlds also allows him to be a psychopomp.

+ Janus—From Roman mythology, Janus is the god of duality, transitions, gateways, doors, time, beginnings and endings, and liminal spaces. He is most often shown as having two faces. The month of January is named after him.

+ Kali Ma—Many may see Kali Ma as a fearful, dark goddess from Hindu mythology, but they're only seeing the destroyer aspect of her being. She's also a creator, protector, and mother figure—a bringer of justice and balance. She is often shown with four arms to reflect her many aspects.

+ Persephone—In the Eleusinian Mysteries, Persephone's descent into and departure from the underworld brings us the changing of the seasons. She rises in spring, bringing life, and journeys back to the underworld in the fall.

Twin Deities Gemini Witches May Be Drawn To:

+ Apollo and Artemis (Greek)
+ Ibeji (Yoruban)
+ Isis and Osiris (Egyptian)

- ✦ Freyr and Freya (Norse)
- ✦ The Divine Twins (Proto-Indo-Europeans)
- ✦ Yama and Yami (Hindu)

Nearly every culture has interesting myths and folklore about twins. I recommend looking up the stories from your own background and practice for more inspiration.

Ritual and Groups

When it comes to ritual, the majority of Gemini witches I know (myself included) are very particular in how we like to do it. We tend to be most confident in situations where we can lead the flow of things, versus being a follower. We feel very comfortable creating a ritual that's improvised, organic, and dynamic, as long as we have the basics down in our wheelhouse. In the right group setting—one that is trustworthy and intellectually and spiritually stimulating for us—we thrive. But we tend to bristle against rigid hierarchy, being told to do things without being told why, and stagnant routines.

Gemini witches excel at adapting to the moment, being able to create something out of nothing. Missing or forgot something? Chances are you'll find a solution to make it work in just a few moments, while others might be distressed or stymied by the challenge. This skill is a feature, not a flaw—though it may be unsettling to others who prefer to stick to a script. It's important to find others who are comfortable working similarly to you if you wish to be part of a coven or form a group. You'll find that things either click right away with others, or it just doesn't happen at all. In the case of the latter, it's best to keep looking for others or do your own thing.

When it comes to designing rituals, I find Gemini witches work best when there's a brief but strong outline to follow and plenty of room for improvisation in between. The anchor or structure points are rooted in considering the following:

- ✦ What's the purpose of the ritual?
- ✦ What is needed to prepare for the ritual?
- ✦ How will it start and how will it end?
- ✦ Who's doing what, where, and when?
- ✦ What will the aftercare look like?

That's just enough to help you plan and stylize the ritual, but not so much planning that it will overload you. Remember, ritual should be a positive and helpful experience!

Divination

When it comes to divination methods, Gemini witches love tools that help us create a story. A really good story is never straightforward—rather, it has twists and turns often signaled by clues found in earlier moments. We're very good at pattern perception—not always the most obvious one that everyone else sees, but rather the underlying or mostly hidden threads. We clue in to symbols and details that others overlook. These minute observations can bring some mighty big muscle to our divination wheelhouse. It's not that we're more psychic than the other signs, but we're picking up on patterns that tend to give us a solid impression of what's going on.

It can be hard though as a Gemini witch to just hang your divination shingle out there without feeling like you have a way to show the work. That's why we often feel more comfortable with physical tools versus straight mediumship. As it's highly visual and symbol-oriented, cartomancy (tarot and oracle cards) is my number one tool for divination. But not just any old deck—it has to be one that visually connects with me and lends itself to the story. I could read accurately with a regular deck of playing cards, but give me a beautifully illustrated deck whose symbolism is carefully considered, and I'm in heaven.

If the theme of a tarot or oracle deck overlaps with another area that you're very interested in, you'll likely find it even more powerful for you. This other area might be a fandom or sub-culture, a particular area of folklore or mythology, or any other niche you're drawn to. That way, you are not only pulling from the system of the tarot or oracle, but also bringing in the additional flavor of something you're knowledgeable about. This deepens not only your own experience, but also the experience of anyone else you might read for.

When it comes to laying out the cards, I personally prefer to keep my spreads simple rather than using more complicated spreads—it keeps the story cleaner and easier to read. You might also find that you're comfortable coming up with your own styles of spreads to suit your needs.

Gemini Balance Tarot or Oracle Spread

Laura Tempest Zakroff

As Geminis, at times it can be hard to tell where our ideas about ourselves end and where what others think of us begins. We can lose touch with who we truly are or be unaware of how we're affecting those around us. This disassociation can cause confusion or send mixed messages to others unintentionally. The Gemini Balance Spread can help you find balance within and without using just four cards. You can use any kind of card system with this spread (tarot, oracle, etc.).

- ◆ Card 1 (left pillar)—how you perceive yourself currently; your strongest attributes
- ◆ Card 2 (right pillar)—how you come off to those around you; their impression and how it may affect you
- ◆ Card 3 (bottom/base)—the underlying factors causing the disconnect or potential barriers
- ◆ Card 4 (top/roof)—what attributes you should nurture or focus on in order to create harmony

Working with Two Decks or Systems Concurrently

Sometimes just one system of divination doesn't give you the full story you're looking for. I mean, face it; you have a tendency to argue with yourself—and agree with both sides simultaneously! Adding in a second system to augment the first one can help clarify matters and create a more definitive picture for you. It's also harder to disagree with!

The question is, which two systems and how? I find that pairing my favorite tarot deck with an oracle deck that suits my mood or the inquiry is a solid method. Some people like to pair up decks by theme or style, so that the images complement each other visually. I tend to go with a supplementary deck that's a bit of a contrast (but not too far off) because I find it feels like consulting two trusted friends who have very different personalities, but both have my best interest at heart. That way you get a slightly different perspective that can give a little more insight. Another option is to pair a set of cards with a completely different system, such as a set of runes, bones, coins, or the Ogham. You could also use a pendulum if you're hoping for a simple yes/no type of clarity, but you might find more help with a symbolic system if you need more details.

With any of these approaches, I suggest pulling one card or item from the secondary tool, rather than doing a whole second spread or casting. There are two ways of consulting with a dual system approach. You can pull from both systems simultaneously, asking the same question, and then compare them. Or you can pull first from your primary system, consider the message, and then go to your secondary system for additional guidance and clarity on what you should know from the first spread. In both approaches, consider and compare how the single element chosen resonates with the initial spread. Ask yourself: What's the overall vibe, and how do the messages sync up? Take a moment to sit with it, and resist the urge to toss everything back, reshuffle, and pull again. You got what you got; work through it.

Tarot Tip from Tempest

Speaking about the tarot, I wanted to add some additional personal perspective to the correspondence chart you'll find in this book on page 123. The system I use to read the tarot assigns the element of air to Wands and the element of fire to Swords. Wands represent ideas, thoughts, and inspiration, while Swords focus on defining, enacting, and setting things into motion. Since Gemini is an air sign, I find that the Wands match up very well in this regard. When I pull the Knight,

Queen, or King of Wands, they tend to signify aspects of myself. As 8, 9, and 10 represent the mutable signs, I see these in Wands as respectively signifying clarity of concept, problem-solving and ingenuity, and conflict resolution, which all tap into Gemini strengths.

MAGICAL
CORRESPONDENCES
Laura Tempest Zakroff

♊

As a Gemini, you'll find that there are certain kinds of spells and magical workings that are right up your alley. Here are some ideas about the types of spells you naturally vibe with, tools that align well with Gemini energy, and some magical ideas for tackling everyday issues as well as larger goals. For example, if you wanted to create a memory charm, you could craft a sigil in your magical journal to aid you. Or you might compose a poem to recite to draw money to you.

Types of Spellcraft

+ Knot Magic
+ Chanting and Breathwork
+ Sigils
+ Wind/Cloud weather work
+ Written petitions
+ Verbal charms

Magical Tools

- Athame or wand, depending on your situation
- Pen and journal
- Feathers
- Incense
- Bells and charms
- Your lungs and voice

Magical Goals and Spell Ideas

- Communication and comprehension magic
- Business and money magic
- Cyber/internet magic
- Memory spells
- Relationship/connectivity magic
- Travel protection and parking spot magic
- Glamour magic

TIMING, PLACES, AND THINGS

Ivo Dominguez, Jr.

Y ou've probably encountered plenty of charts and lists in books and online, cataloging which things relate to your Sun sign and ruling planet. There are many gorgeously curated assortments of herbs, crystals, music playlists, fashions, sports, fictional characters, tarot cards, and more that are assigned to your Sun sign. These compilations of associations are more than a curiosity or for entertainment. Correspondences are like treasure maps to show you where to find the type and flavor of power you are seeking. Correspondences are flowcharts and diagrams that show the inner occult relationship between subtle energies and the physical world. Although there are many purposes for lists of correspondences, there are two that are especially valuable to becoming a better Gemini witch.

• • • • •

The first is to contemplate the meaning of the correspondences, the ways in which they reveal meaningful details about your Sun sign and ruling planet, and how they connect to you. This will deepen your understanding of what it is to be a Gemini witch.

The second is to use these items as points of connection to access energies and essences that support your witchcraft. This will expand the number of tools and resources at your disposal for all your efforts.

Each of the sections in this chapter will introduce you to a type of correlation with suggestions on how to identify and use it. These are just starting points, and you will find many more as you explore and learn. As you broaden your knowledge, you may find yourself a little bit confused as you find that sources disagree on the correlations. These contradictions are generally not a matter of who is in error but a matter of perspective, cultural differences, and the intended uses for the correlations. Anything that exists in the physical world can be described as a mixture of all the elements, planets, and signs. You may be a Gemini, but depending on the rest of your chart, there may be strong concentrations of other signs and elements. For example, if you find that a particular herb is listed as associated with both Gemini and Libra, it is because it contains both natures in abundance. In the cases of strong multiple correlations, it is important to summon or tune in to the one you need.

Times

You always have access to your power as a Gemini witch, but there are times when the flow is stronger, readily available, or more easily summoned. There are sophisticated astrological methods to select dates and times that are specific to your birth chart. Unless you want to learn quite a bit more astrology or hire someone to determine these for you, you can do quite well with simpler methods. Let's look at the cycles of the solar year, the lunar month, and the hours of day-night rotation. When the Sun is in Gemini, or the Moon is in Gemini, or late in the morning every day, you are in the sweet spot for tuning in to the core of your power.

Gemini season is roughly May 21–June 20, but check your astrological calendar or ephemeris to determine when it is for a specific year in your time zone. The amount of accessible energy is highest when the Sun is at the same degree of Gemini as it is in your birth chart. This peak will not always be on your birth date, but very close to it. Take advantage of Gemini season for working magick and for recharging and storing up energy for the whole year.

The Moon moves through the twelve signs every lunar cycle and spends around two and half days in each sign. When the Moon is in Gemini, you have access to more lunar power because the Moon in the heavens has a resonant link to the Sun in your birth chart. At some point during its time in Gemini, the Moon will be at the same degree as your Sun. For you, that will be the peak of the energy during the Moon's passage through Gemini that month. While the Moon is in Gemini, your psychism is stronger, as is your ability to manifest things. When the Moon is in its waxing gibbous phase in any sign, you can draw upon its power more readily because it is resonant to your sign.

There are no holidays during Gemini season like an equinox, solstice, or cross-quarter day. However, the peak of Gemini season is its midpoint at the 15th degree; this is a special day of power for you. You can look up when the Sun is in the 15th degree of Gemini for the current or future years using online resources or an ephemeris. Gemini is the third sign of the zodiac, and the zodiac is like a clock for the purpose of spellwork. Late morning corresponds to the airy power of Gemini. If you are detail focused, you might be wondering when late morning is. This varies with the time of year and with your location, but if you must have a time, think of it as 10:00 a.m. to 12:00 p.m. Or you can use your intuition and feel your way to when late morning is on any given day. The powers that flow during this time are rich, creative, and filled with possibilities for you to experience. Plan on using the Gemini energy of the midmorning to fuel and feed spells for learning, divination, creativity, and new growth.

The effect of these special times can be joined in any combination. For example, you can choose to do work at late morning when the Moon is in Gemini, or when the Sun is in Gemini at late morning, or when the Moon is in Gemini during Gemini season. You can combine all three as well. Each of these time period groupings will have a distinctive feeling. Experiment and use your instincts to discover how to use these in your work.

Places

There are activities, professions, phenomena, and behaviors that have an affinity, a resonant connection, to Gemini and its ruling planet, Mercury. These activities occur in the locations that suit or facilitate their expressions. There is magick to be claimed from those places that is earmarked for Gemini or your ruling planet of Mercury. Just like your birth chart, the world around you contains the influences of all the planets and signs, but in different proportions and arrangements. You can always draw upon Gemini or Mercury energy, though there are times when it is more abundant depending on astrological considerations. Places and spaces have energies that accumulate and can be tapped as well. Places contain the physical, emotional, and spiritual environments that are created by the actions of the material objects, plants, animals, and people occupying those spaces. Some of the interactions between these things can generate or concentrate the energies and patterns that can be used by Gemini witches.

If you look at traditional astrology books, you'll find listings of places assigned to Gemini and Mercury that include locations such as these:

- ◎ Libraries, schools, and studios
- ◎ Bus stops, airports, and train stations
- ◎ Highways, walking paths, and crossroads
- ◎ Marketplaces, town halls, places where people gather

These are very clearly linked to the themes associated with Gemini and Mercury. With a bit of brainstorming and free-associating, you'll find many other less obvious locations and situations where you can draw upon this power. For example, online immersive environments, chat rooms, and museums can produce a current you can plug into. Any mentally stimulating activity, having a discussion, composing a message, or similar activities can become a source of power for a Gemini witch. All implements or actions related to travel, enjoying any of the arts, multitasking, energetic social settings, and many more situations also could be a source for energy.

While you can certainly go to places that are identified as locations where Gemini and/or Mercury energy is plentiful to do workings, you can find those energies in many other circumstances. Don't be limited by the idea that the places must be the ones that have a formalized link to Gemini. Be on the lookout for Gemini or Mercury themes and activities wherever you may be. Remember that people thinking, feeling, or participating in activities connected to your sign and its ruling planet are raising power. If you can identify with it as resonating with your Sun sign or ruling planet, then you can call the power and put it to use. You complete the circuit to engage the flow with your visualization, intentions, and actions.

Plants

Gemini is airy, intellectual, and quick in motion, and its color is pale yellow and orange (though most pastels work). Mercury overlaps with these but also adds a focus on mechanical knowledge, work with your peers, physical skills that use dexterity, and the impartial perspective of a neutral polarity. Herbs, resins, oils, fruits, vegetables, woods, and flowers that strongly exhibit one or more of these qualities can be called upon to support your magic. Here are a few examples:

- ◎ Rosemary because of its stimulating scent and mind-boosting power.

- ◎ Lavender because it soothes a mind that is running too fast.

- ◎ Cinquefoil for being so versatile and especially for helping with commerce.

- ◎ Mullein for protection in travel, healing the lungs, and a myriad of uses.

- ◎ Dill because it calms the emotion but clears the mind and protects against illusions.

Once you understand the rationale for making these assignments, the lists of correspondences will make more sense. Another thing to consider is that each part of a plant may resonate more strongly with a different element, planet, and sign. Mullein shows its connection with Gemini and Mercury through its pale yellow flowers and its use in travel magick. However, mullein is also used in fire magick as a candle for the dead and grows slowly in marginal places that are Saturnian. Which energy steps forward depends on your call and invitation. Like calls to like is a truism in witchcraft. When you use your Gemini nature to make a call, you are answered by the Gemini part of the plant.

Plant materials can take the form of incense, anointing oils, altar pieces, potions, washes, magickal implements, foods, flower arrangements, and so on. The mere presence of plant material that is linked to Gemini or

Mercury will be helpful to you. However, to gain the most benefit from plant energy, you need to actively engage with it. Push some of your energy into the plants and then pull on it to start the flow. Although much of the plant material you work with will be dried or preserved, it retains a connection to living members of their species. You may also want to reach out and try to commune with the spirit, the group soul, of the plants to request their assistance or guidance. This will awaken the power slumbering in the dried or preserved plant material. Spending time with living plants, whether they be houseplants, in your yard, or in a public garden will strengthen your conversation with the green beings under Gemini's eye.

Crystals and Stones

Before digging into this topic, let's clear up some of the confusion around the birthstones for the signs of the zodiac. There are many varying lists for birthstones. Also be aware that some are related to the calendar month rather than the zodiacal signs. There are traditional lists, but the most commonly available lists for birthstones were created by jewelers to sell more jewelry. Also be cautious of the word *traditional* as some jewelers refer to the older lists compiled by jewelers as "traditional." The traditional lists created by magickal practitioners also diverge from each other because of cultural differences and the availability of different stones in the times and places the lists were created. If you have already formed a strong connection to a birthstone that you discover is not really connected to the energy of your sign, keep using it. Your connection is proof of its value to you in moving, holding, and shifting energy, whether or not it is specifically attuned to Gemini.

These are my preferred assignments of birthstones for the signs of the zodiac:

Aries	Bloodstone, Carnelian, Diamond
Taurus	Rose Quartz, Amber, Sapphire
Gemini	Agate, Tiger's Eyes, Citrine
Cancer	Moonstone, Pearl, Emerald
Leo	Heliodor, Peridot, Black Onyx
Virgo	Green Aventurine, Moss Agate, Zircon
Libra	Jade, Lapis Lazuli, Labradorite
Scorpio	Obsidian, Pale Beryl, Nuummite
Sagittarius	Turquoise, Blue Topaz, Iolite

Capricorn	Black Tourmaline, Howlite, Ruby
Aquarius	Amethyst, Sugalite, Garnet
Pisces	Ametrine, Smoky Quartz, Aquamarine

There are many other possibilities that work just as well, and I suggest you find what responds best for you as an individual. I've included all twelve signs in case you'd like to use the stones for your Moon sign or rising sign. Hands-on experimentation is the best approach, so I suggest visiting crystal or metaphysical shops and rock and mineral shows when possible. Here's some information on the three I prefer for Gemini:

Agate
If you know anything about agates, your first question will be which one. The answer is the one you need. Agates come in a wide range of colors and patterns. A Gemini's energy is highly changeable, and your interests are diverse. Agates help keep you in the zone and connected to the flow of whatever you are doing. They ground you without bringing you down. They also help keep your energy in harmony with whatever you are doing. Explore the agate family until you find your favorite set of agates. I suggest you start with blue lace agate as it is gentle and accessible.

Tiger's Eye

Although there is an emphasis on the mind for Geminis, the emotions matter as well. Tiger's eye helps support and maintain self-confidence as you go through changes. It sharpens your perceptions, both physical and psychic, and clear perception is essential for Gemini well-being. Boldness and certainty are encouraged by this stone and a good counterbalance to the indecisiveness that can come from seeing too many sides of each question. Tiger's eye also helps when you are processing fear or trying to eliminate toxic emotions. There are several colors common to tiger's eye. The bluish tiger's eye is more calming. The reddish tiger's eye increases motivation. The golden tiger's eye stabilizes the mind.

Citrine

Citrine inspires joy and optimism and helps you see your good traits and abilities. It helps keep you centered so you don't wobble or zoom off course when you are going full speed. Your mind will skip around less and stay on task. This stone helps you direct your energies and intentions earthward for drawing material abundance into your life. Citrine is also good at sparking new ideas and fresh insights when you are having a creative block. If you have been too rushed to eat well or rest enough, use the energy of citrine to nudge you to make healthier choices.

Intuition and spiritual guidance play a part in the making of correlations and, in the case of traditional lore, the collective experience of many generations of practitioners. There is also reasoning behind how these assignments are made, and understanding the process will help you choose well. Here are some examples of this reasoning:

- ◎ Crystals assigned to Gemini are light, cheerful colors or come in many varieties because they suggest Gemini and Mercury in their changeable appearance.

- ◎ Gemini's metal is mercury, a liquid metal that changes shape and conducts electricity. It is a highly toxic metal, so aluminum or platinum are its substitutes in most uses. Aluminum is lightweight, melts easily, and conducts electricity. Platinum is said to have both lunar and solar qualities, so it is a version of the twins of Gemini. Crystals that have significant amounts of aluminum, such as blue kyanite, dumortierite, and alexandrite, also work well for you.

- ◎ Crystals such as lepidolite, larimar, and yellow jasper, whose lore and uses are related to Gemini or Mercury actions or topics such as communication, travel, and creativity, are recommended as crystals for Gemini.

◎ Crystals that are the opposite of the themes for Gemini provide a counterbalance to an excessive manifestation of Gemini traits. For example, citrine appears on lists of crystals for many other signs but is useful for Gemini for its centering and focusing effect.

◎ Crystals suggested for Sagittarius, your opposite sign, are also useful to maintain your balance.

Working with Ritual Objects

A substantial number of traditions or schools of witchcraft use magickal tools that are consecrated to represent and hold the power of the elements. Oftentimes in these systems, there is one primary tool for each of the elements and other tools that are alternatives to these or are mixtures of elements. There are many possible combinations and reasons for why the elements are assigned to different tools in different traditions, and they all work within their own context. Find and follow what works best for you.

Magickal tools and ritual objects are typically cleansed, consecrated, and charged to prepare them for use. In addition to following whatever procedure you may have for preparing your tools, add in a step to incorporate your energy and identity as a Gemini witch. This is especially productive for magickal tools and ritual objects that are connected to air or are used for centering work or to store or focus power. By adding Gemini energy and patterning into the preparation of your tools, you will find it easier to raise, move, and shape energy with them in your workings.

There are many magickal tools and ritual objects that do not have any attachment to specific elements. The core of your life force and magickal power springs from your Gemini Sun. So, when you consciously join your awareness of your Gemini core with the power flowing through the tools or objects, it increases their effectiveness. Develop the habit of using the name *Gemini* as a word of power, the glyph for Gemini for summoning power, and the pale colors or orange of Gemini to visualize its flow. Whether it be a pendulum, a wand, a crystal, or a chalice, your Gemini energy will be quick to rise and answer your call.

A Charging Practice

When you consciously use your Gemini witch energy to send power into tools, it tunes them more closely to your aura. Here's a quick method for imbuing any tool with your Gemini energy.

1. Place the tool in front of you on a table or altar.
2. Take a breath in, imagining that you are breathing in light yellow energy, and then say "Gemini" as you exhale. Repeat this three times.
3. Lift up your forearms so they form two parallel vertical lines. Now move your forearms so they are parallel and horizontal to each other. You've just formed the glyph for Gemini.
4. Now, using a finger, trace the glyph of Gemini over or on the tool you are charging. Repeat this several times and imagine the glyph being absorbed by the tool.
5. Pick up the tool, take in a breath while imaging pale yellow energy, and blow that charged breath over the tool.

Timing, Places, and Things

6. Say "Blessed be!" and proceed with using the tool or putting it away.

Hopefully this charging practice will inspire you and encourage you to experiment. Develop the habit of using the name *Gemini* as a word of power, the glyph for Gemini for summoning power, and the colors of Gemini to visualize its flow. Feel free to use these spontaneously in all your workings. Whether it be a pendulum, a wand, a crystal, a chalice, a ritual robe, or anything else that catches your imagination, these simple methods can have a large impact. The Gemini energy you imprint into them will be quick to rise and answer your call.

Crystal Clarity Spell
for a Gemini Witch

Najah Lightfoot

Gemini. Ruled by the planet Mercury. Quick-witted, intelligent, super smart, versatile, adaptable. These are our positive traits. Easily bored, easily irritated, and frustrated. Quick to rage, but slow to anger. Will burn you quickly but then want to apply a bandage. Loyal but can be unforgiving. Can think forward and backward at the same time. Highly intuitive and sensitive.

Whoa! Being the twins of the zodiac is exhausting! A Gemini witch has so much going on in their minds. We are highly extroverted yet deeply introverted at the same time. All this mental fortitude can wear us out, break us down, cause us to weep uncontrollably, then to smile a day later.

No wonder we need spaces—places where we can recharge, quiet our brains and our minds, find the relief and respite of crystal clarity. This spell specifically written for Gemini witches will help slow you down, take a breather, and focus. It will help you stop fidgeting and simply be in the now, without distractions from that thing over there we've just got to look at. How do I know this? Because I am a quintessential Mercurial Gemini! That's right. Born in the month of May, shortly after the season of Gemini begins. And obviously I'm a writer, too, which is good for my Gemini brain.

Location, location, location! Choose a spot where you will be undisturbed. If you can be outside, all the better. As an air sign, fresh air is essential. In the fresh air, we can breathe and relax.

You will need:
+ White candle
+ Fireproof candleholder
+ Clear quartz crystal

Instructions:
For this spell, gather your white candle and your clear quartz crystal. Clear quartz is the master candle of crystals. Clear quartz is a conduit for clarity, focus, and amplifying your intentions.

Place your white candle in a fireproof candleholder. Light the candle. Say, "Blessed be element of fire. Fire that lights the way of clarity for me."

Hold your clear quartz crystal at eye level. Gaze into the crystal. Stare into the crystal until you feel yourself begin to relax. Close your eyes and allow any images or thoughts to wash over and through you. When you feel ready, open your eyes and view the world with your newfound clarity. Extinguish the candle either by snuffing or pinching it out. Keep your white candle and crystal together in a place where you can easily gather them to use again anytime you feel the need to repeat this spell.

HERBAL
CORRESPONDENCES

♊

These plant materials all have a special connection to your energy as a Gemini witch. There are many more, but these are a good starting point.

Herbs	
Elecampane	banish negative beings, trance work, focus your power
Fenugreek	brings luck, money drawing, anchors intention
Yarrow	soul protector, divination, see beyond deceptions

Flowers

Lily of the Valley	summoning, opens higher planes, optimim
Sweet Pea	strength, honesty, communion with nature spirits
California Poppy	reduce stress, reveal spirits, pro-phetic dreams

Incense and Fragrances

White Sandalwood	meditation, attracts positivity, calls the divine
Mastic	unites differences, improves learn-ing, increases concentration
Lemongrass	opens psychic gifts, clarity of purpose, divination

CLEANSING AND SHIELDING

Laura Tempest Zakroff

When we think of good hygiene, we tend to think of cleaning the physical body. But good hygiene practice also extends to our spiritual, emotional, and mental selves. Cleansing and clearing out toxic energy are important for keeping us healthy. These practices apply not only to your body, but to your space as well. It helps immensely to minimize our exposure by taking preventative measures that protect and shield us. As inventor, writer, and diplomat Benjamin Franklin once said, "An ounce of prevention is worth a pound of cure." This is especially true for energetic cleansing and protection. Especially since as Geminis, we are more drawn to small tasks versus performing big elaborate ordeals. Not that we don't like the fancy and theatrical in theory, but in the execution of actually doing the thing, we're more successful in doing the quick and accessible. In this section, we'll go over some simple methods you'll find helpful as a Gemini to maintain effective metaphysical hygiene.

You can work with the elements in a variety of ways to clear and protect yourself and your space—either by themselves or in combination. For example, burning incense is technically a combination of using fire (the flame), earth (the incense), and air (the smoke). A cleansing bath may involve herbs and salt in addition to water, and it takes heat to make the water warm. Also consider that the elements can be used to both clear out unwanted energy as well as bring in desired energy. Think of the process like a using a whiteboard—you wipe down what's no longer needed, creating a clean surface. Then you add your own information with markers of your choosing. The key is focusing your intent as you do the work.

Air It Out

Geminis tend to have sensitive lungs, so we tend to be very much aware of scent, air quality, and how our breathing is affected. Therefore, air can have a powerful impact on ourselves and our spaces. Cleansing with smoke and building with scent are generally pretty fast and easy to do as well.

Smoke cleansing is pretty much exactly what it sounds like—clearing an area of unwanted energy through the power of smoke. Just like vacuuming, but no need to plug anything in or loud noise to scare the animals! If I'm looking to really clear out a space, I'll make an herb bundle wand out of what's local to me. When I lived in Seattle, there was a giant cedar tree just down the street. Here in New England, I look to my garden, where I have mugwort, sage, lavender, and rosemary all within easy reach. The mugwort especially grows fast and plentiful and is easy to dry. If you don't have a garden or an area nearby where you can wildcraft, it is certainly not the end of the world (nor a ding on your witch card) to shop the herb section of your local grocery store. Simply bless the procured herbs as you prepare the bundle. To make an herb wand, all you need to do is gather a small spray of herbs (about six to eight inches in length, stems intact), wrap them together with natural threads, and hang the bundle up somewhere safe to dry. When you're ready to burn it, simply light one end and then gently extinguish the flame with your breath so that it will smolder and smoke. When doing this type of clearing on an environment, I will walk counterclockwise around the space three times. If clearing my body (or someone else's), I like to put the smoldering wand in a small cauldron and stand in front of or over it, waving the smoke up over and past the body.

So, smoke cleansing is great for removing unwanted energy, but what about bringing in desired energy and creating a special atmosphere? This is where incense excels. If I'm looking to simply shift the energy of the room or myself, I'll burn some incense. For bringing in energy to change a space, I tend to move in a clockwise motion, usually at least three cycles around. I may also draw sigils in the air at windows and doors for extra protection. This method works exceptionally well when you need your wards of protection to be invisible. The main things to consider when burning incense are how you want the space to feel, what mood are you looking for, and what you wish to draw into the space.

I love a good incense, but I'm very particular about what I burn and for how long. I like the good solid basics like sandalwood, frankincense, and nag champa—all usually easy to find in stick or cone form. They each produce a pleasant earthy smell that isn't too heavy and creates a positive atmosphere. Currently, my favorite quick incenses are loose blends from my friends at The Veiled Crow;[2] all you need to do is light the incense itself in a firesafe bowl, and it produces a fabulous smoke that burns for just a few minutes if you do a small amount. No charcoal block needed! You can also make your own incense blends fairly easily from herbs and resins if you don't mind using a bit of elbow grease and enjoy hunting down ingredients.

Even if you're allergic or highly sensitive to smoke and incense, you can still benefit from utilizing air to clear a space in other ways. If smoke is the main irritant, then you can use a clearing or blessing spray instead. These are tinctures (herb or oil-infused liquids) in handy spray bottles. They are easily

---

2. Visit them at https://www.veiledcrow.com/.

available online from most witchy shops, or you can make your own. Simply mist the space or body to use. If the issue is scent, then you can't go wrong with simply opening some windows and bringing in fresh air. In fact, this is something I do anyway whether I'm using smoke, incense, or a spray. Ideally open at least two windows at opposite ends of your space to create a draft so the air is pulled through the space. You can also use a small fan to help it along. If it's a very cold day, you don't have to do this for very long; even just a few minutes will do, and I guarantee you'll notice the difference.

The Water Way

Air is definitely a solid go-to when you need to do a quick clearing that doesn't take a lot of time or effort. But there are other ways of clearing that are still pretty easy, even if they involve a little more time and effort. When I need to drastically shift the energy of a space or my mood, I turn to water.

I have a lot of cauldrons (which tends to happen if you write a book about them I guess), and folks often ask me which is my favorite. Hands down, it's my bathtub. I not only use it for mundanely cleaning my body, but it's also ideal for cleansing, healing, blessing, and other magical work. I also love that bath or shower work is very simple, but I could definitely add more dressing if I'm in the mood, such as candles, incense, special salts and tinctures, and so on. For a very simple clearing, just water and a handful of sea salt will do the trick. If you have a connection with a local body of water or special well and have collected a vial of water from it, you could also add a few drops to the mix. If I'm looking to reset myself, I'll fill up a muslin bag with some herbs from my garden, including rose petals or rosehips, mugwort, lavender, and whatever else may be appropriate for the working. I use the bag instead of sprinkling leaves and petals directly in the water because, while it looks pretty, the last thing I want to do after doing a blessing or cleansing bath is have a hefty job of cleaning out the tub or worrying about my plumbing. Also, before adding any herbs to your bath, be sure to check to see if there are any possible health concerns you should be aware of to avoid allergic reactions or other issues.

On the more mundane side of things—but in my opinion just as important and powerful when it comes to clearing—is physically cleaning a space. If I'm feeling out of sorts, often all I need to do is look to what's going on in my house to effect some change. It doesn't have to be the whole house or even a whole room—sometimes just my desk or the bathroom sink will do the trick. I find this helps clear the mind while also giving me a very physical means of affecting my immediate world. Add a little blessed water to what you're scrubbing, mopping, or spraying, and you've included a touch of magic to the task.

Lastly, while not exactly water, a process that certainly involves liquid magic is anointing with oil. Applying a little oil to your wrists, neck, and/or breastbone is a great way to add a layer of daily protection. If you're unsure of where to start, try a flower essence that taps into both Gemini and the month you were born:

- ⊙ May Gemini—Lily of the Valley, Hawthorn
- ⊙ June Gemini—Rose, Honeysuckle

These flowers are known for blooming in your birth month and are quite fragrant. If the time of year is right, collect some blossoms on your birthday and make an oil infusion or tincture and use it throughout the year.

The Power of Shiny Things

How we dress and adorn ourselves allows us to try out ideas and explore identity. We tend not to have one particular style, but multiple styles we prefer. After all, we Geminis contain multitudes! Plus, there's a lot of magic to consider in how we adorn ourselves. Glamour magic is all about changing not only how others perceive us, but how we feel about ourselves. Adding elements of protection brings another powerful layer to the ensemble. Not only are you adorning yourself aesthetically, but you're also adding a shield of protection.

When I was a teenager, I read an article about Geminis that said we "have a tendency toward excessive adornment." I looked down at my hands covered in silver rings and thought,

"Define excessive, because all of this is necessary!" Coco Chanel is rumored to have said, "Before you leave the house, look in the mirror and take at least one thing off." That's never sat well with me. While it's true that looking in the mirror before leaving the house is a good rule of thumb, I'm more of the mind to add at least one more thing—and making sure it's an item of power and significance to me. There are certain things I never leave the house without wearing: a consecrated necklace and at least one "evil eye bracelet."

The initial power and significance can come from where you got the item—maybe it was a gift from a loved one, a hard-earned reward for yourself, or from a special place or trip. I believe that simply wearing that item builds a level of power and protection, but you can always take additional steps to infuse it with specific energy by blessing or consecrating it.

A Shining Shield

This is a simple working to charge a piece of jewelry with the task of being a portable shield.

You will need:

+ Representatives of the elements: a small bowl of water, some salt or earth, your favorite incense, and a small candle.
+ A piece of jewelry: I recommend selecting one you can wear on your body every day without irritation, such as a simple ring, a small pendant, or a pin made of silver, gold, or a similar high-quality metal.

To tap into your Gemini essence, you can perform this spell when the full Moon or new Moon is in Gemini.

1. Set up your working space with elements ready—candle lit and incense smoking.
2. Pick up the jewelry and pass it through the smoke, saying, "I charge this [item] with the power of air to protect me from ill winds and negative thoughts."

3. Next, carefully pass the jewelry through the flame, saying, "I charge this [item] with the power of fire to burn away all that would do me harm."

4. Now dip the jewelry in the bowl of water, saying, "I charge this [item] with the power of water to wash away potential threats and unwanted energy."

5. Next, rest the jewelry in your earth element and say, "I charge this [item] with the power of earth to bring solidity and strength to my shield."

6. Lastly, you can also ask a deity, spirit, or ancestor for additional protection by saying, "Using this [item] as a guide, I ask that [name of entity] watch over and guide me as I wear this shining shield. So mote it be."

You can bless multiple items in this way and recharge them on a regular basis if you feel you need to. You can do this by repeating the spell again, but placing the item on your altar when you're not wearing it is also a good method.

WHAT SETS A GEMINI OFF, AND HOW TO RECOVER

Laura Tempest Zakroff

One quick way to get a Gemini riled up is to present us with information we know is wrong. Whether it's being told to us or it's something we're observing happening to someone else, our gut instinct is to fix it. NOW. But that's not always the best course of action for our sanity and overall well-being.

You might have seen the online XKCD cartoon titled "Duty Calls."[3] If not, it's a single black-and-white frame depicting a stick figure sitting at a desk in front of their computer. There's a dialogue happening between the person and someone else out of frame, whom their back is toward. The latter asks, "Are you coming to bed?" The person sitting at their desk responds, "I can't. This is important." The other

---

3. XKCD, "Duty Calls," XKCD, accessed October 31, 2022, https://xkcd.com/386/.

person asks, "What?" They reply, "Someone is *wrong* on the internet."

I'm sure at some point you too have been this person. One of the most difficult things for me to deal with as a Gemini witch is the propagation of misinformation. My natural default state is "let me tell you ALL THE THINGS," not because I want to show off what I know, but because I'm passionate about sharing information that could be helpful for others. So, the passing along of inconsistent, inaccurate, or just plain incorrect data drives me bonkers. I can be overcome with this urge to address the misunderstanding and get the right info out there instead.

What qualifies as misinformation when it comes to witchcraft? It could be making generalizations that are more harmful than helpful, such as about certain groups, cultures, or traditions. Or giving instructions that could be dangerous to inexperienced practitioners, such as fire hazards or the improper use of baneful herbs that could lead to sickness or death if used incorrectly. The posting of biased or misleading information about other witches or practices primarily to stir up drama is another one.

How to Avoid the Bait

I used to get rather worked up about it, meaning I'd instantly take to the keyboard in order to right the wrong. But I've learned to chill out instead and watch the waves of information as they go by. I have found it is better to not react immediately and instead to observe and scope out what's happening as it develops. This pause in approach helps me form a better opinion of the situation and perhaps offer insight that will be more helpful or harmonious.

With any kind of news or release of info, there's a type of pendulum effect that will happen. At first with the introduction of the new material, everything swings hard one way. Then you'll find that opinion will swing hard in the opposite direction. Then within a few days, a middle ground is found between the two extremes, often resolving the discrepancies and incorporating differing opinions in a more balanced way.

For example, let's say the trending concept is a humorous blog post on "Why Cats Make the Best Familiars." It will get a slew of responses along the lines of "THEY DO!!" and then eventually someone will come up with a response of "Cats Are NOT the Best Familiars and Here's Why" along with someone else writing "Why Your Cat Isn't Your Familiar and What Else Is Wrong with Your Practice." Everyone gets worked up about it. Eventually the trend will get to a place where someone will present a thoughtful piece that talks about the history of familiars, maybe includes both historic and contemporary references, and acknowledges that we all have strong feelings about our relationships with our pets, magical or not. Reason and context are applied in a more considerate manner and, basically, cooler heads prevail. And then everyone moves on to the next thing, as they always do.

It can be fun to get caught up in the moment, riding the pendulum as it swings, but it can also be equally as stressful and taxing. Going on the offense to correct an idea eventually migrates to finding yourself having to work defense instead. It's better to tap into some of your other Gemini strengths, such as the ability to consider multiple viewpoints and playing with multiple strategies mentally rather than shooting instantly from the hip. Rather than joining the fray, use the opportunity to bring a deeper sense of understanding and harmony to the situation. Just remember to be respectful of others' feelings in how you phrase what you write or say. Also, if Mercury is in retrograde, you'll want to be extra mindful of possible miscommunication. Even with the best intentions, things can easily go awry during these times.

Is This the Right Time?

Sometimes you won't be able to add directly to a conversation or discourse. What do you do then? First, it's good to know if it's even your place or best prerogative to step in. Sometimes it's just not your job to add in your two cents. You especially don't want to speak for or especially *over* others whose voices are often disenfranchised, ignored, or otherwise overlooked.

Do what you can to direct focus to those folks in order to amplify their voices. Another thing to consider is that maybe you're not as informed about a topic as you might think you are. Be honest with yourself and take a back seat to the conversation so you can get better informed.

But what if it *does* concern you? Very directly? What then? As an author, one of the most frustrating things for me personally are reviews that don't accurately reflect the nature of the work. I know, I know, they always tell you that you shouldn't read the reviews. But Geminis are just so darn curious (and information obsessed) by nature that it's hard to not take a peek to see how a work is being received. You tend to see a bit of everything (and everyone) when you put your work out into the world, and there's very little you can do about its reception once it's out there. Having trained as a visual artist and designer, I'm well versed in the critique process—both in giving and receiving constructive critique. But book reviews tend to be a whole other animal entirely. While there are professional reviewers out there, the majority of folks are simply sharing their feelings and opinions however they want—which is totally fine! These tend to center more around someone's feelings than being interested in giving information that an author could use constructively in the future. Not to say that all negative feedback is bad or ill-intentioned, as sometimes you can learn how to do something better by considering things that make you uncomfortable. There's always room for improvement, especially when it's given in a respectful light. But it can be really frustrating when someone—for whatever reason—misunderstands or misrepresents you/your work in their review or is even downright abusive or nasty.

Putting It All into Perspective

So how do I deal with that kind of negativity emotionally and mentally? My best solution is to consider that a review often says more about the reader than it does you or the work itself. Their words can give insight into what that person is excited by or fearful of, their level of experience (or lack thereof), and their general state of being. It helps to remember that there's still a person at the other end of those words, even if they're not giving you the same courtesy or recognition. It's easy to feel anonymous or antipathic behind a screen (some even find perceived power in that position), but there's still a human being on both sides of the equation.

Sometimes it also helps to have a bit of teamwork going on to process ideas and thoughts. If something does manage to get under my skin, I talk to my partner about it. I find this helps alleviate some of the stress by talking it out with someone I trust and who knows me and my work. Another friend who is also a Gemini witch and author has an agreement with their partner regarding reviews. Their partner is the one who reads the reviews and then filters through the content that is most helpful. That doesn't mean she gives her only the good bits, but she can spare her partner unnecessary stress when people are excessively rude or bigoted in their reviews.

What if you're not an author, artist, musician, poet, or other creative whose work is often subjected to reviews? Consider applying my advice to other areas where you may find yourself being scrutinized or criticized, such as a work or family situation. What's going on with the other person and their life right now? Can you have a conversation to clear things up? If not, is it something you want to direct your energy to, or are you better off ignoring it? You can waste a lot of time and energy trying to defend yourself against someone who is not interested in hearing your side of the story regardless. If it's not a person or situation you care about or are invested in, might be best to say no and move on.

Remember, it's not your job to fix all the misinformation out there. Value your time and energy by choosing your battles wisely. Not only will your stress levels drop, but you'll be able to spend more time focusing on what you love and wish to invest in. Always a win!

The Silver-Tongue Gemini Spell

Irene Glasse

Geminis are blessed with communication skills, but even we can use a boost from time to time. My Gemini nature manifests in my community work—I frequently work as part of a team. Sometimes that means I need to persuade others to follow my lead. In those moments, I lean heavily on my Gemini communication skills. Perform this spell when you need to convince others of your point of view. It is designed to enhance your natural gifts.

You will need:

+ One small silver craft bell on a string or chain long enough to be placed over the head and worn like a necklace

+ White sandalwood incense, matches/lighter, and an incense burner

+ One cup of tea that is both sweet and spicy (chai, honey-ginger, and fruity "zinger" teas will all work well here)

Instructions:

This spell is most effectively performed on a Wednesday during the
planetary hour of Mercury. Assem-
ble your supplies and cast sacred
space if so desired.

Begin by offering incense to a deity
associated with communication or gifted
with poetry in the pantheon you work with the
most. Some examples are Bragi or Odhinn (Norse), Iris or
Hermes (Greek), Ogma (Celtic), and Papa Legba (Vodou).
If you do not work regularly with a specific pantheon, offer
the incense to Gemini's ruling planet and deity, Mercury
(Roman).

As you light the incense, say,

Hail, oh shining one, teller of tales
Hail, oh traveler, swift on the trails
Sweet is the sound of your sacred song
Be with me now to make this spell strong
Incense I offer to hallow the air
Presented to you along with this prayer
Hail, [deity name]!

Pick up the bell and cup it in both hands. Hold it over the tea and gently shake your cupped hands to make the bell jingle. Say,

Bright and silver, smooth and clear
When this bell's sweet song I hear
My voice rings with persuasive power
From the first tone for one full hour
Silver-tongued I shall be
My words flowing smooth and easily

Put on the bell necklace, feeling the connection of the bell near your throat chakra, the seat of communication.

Visualize yourself gifted with persuasive power. Imagine scenarios where people listen to you and are swayed by your words. Consider how it will feel to use language so effectively. When your visualization is clear and detailed, begin to raise energy in a way appropriate for you (breathing exercises, dance, song, or chant). When you feel like you cannot hold more energy within you, blow the visualization into the cup of tea. This may take more than one breath to do. Pick up the cup of tea and say,

Eloquence flow into me
Sweet and spicy as this tea
Touch my lips and tongue with skill
Persuasive power I now instill

To kindle brighter when I hear
The silver bell here ringing clear

Drink the tea, taking time to savor the taste. As you do so, visualize the power you raised flowing into you and gifting you with eloquence.

Release your circle and place the bell somewhere safe. When you need to tap into the power of language for persuasion, jingle the bell before starting your conversation. It will act as the spark to set the enchantment in motion.

A BRIEF BIO OF DOLORES ASHCROFT-NOWICKI

* * *

Tiffany Lazic

Do you know that feeling you have when you accidentally stumble upon something that has been there all along, just below your sightline, and it is such a blinding revelation that you wonder how you ever existed before that unveiling? Discovering Dolores Ashcroft-Nowicki was that experience for me.

Born in 1929, this remarkable esoteric teacher seems to have been kissed by the liminal right from the start. Being raised on Jersey Island—UK influenced but not controlled off the coast of France, but "belonging" to neither—cannot help but be ideal gestational ground for a Gemini spirit. With her Roma ancestry and parents, who were themselves open to the occult sciences, Dolores was raised with a potent intersection of magical nature and esoteric nurture. It seems inevitable that her curious mind and seeking spirit would, in the 1960s, lead her to the work of Dion Fortune and the Fraternity of the Inner Light. She left the Fraternity in good standing after a number of years to work with two other significant pillars of the esoteric tradition, W. E. Butler and Gareth Knight, on what would eventually become the Servants of the Light school. In 1976, she became the Director of Studies of SOL, a position she held until a few years ago, solidly in her nineties and still teaching.

I would not presume to know what Dolores's message is through her life's work, but, if the Gemini mind can be summed up in two words—a minimalist task that, by the way, is torturous and near impossible for any Gemini—it is through that most infamous of Greek axioms: *know thyself* (*gnothi sauton*). Ever questing. Ever inquisitive. Looking for patterns and meaning, structure and synchronicities that bring awareness and understanding ever deeper. Geminis tend not to skim the surface or get stuck in the weeds—for very long, anyways. They seek out the interconnecting paths, joyfully exploring the intersecting elements, more often than not coming to brilliant kaleidoscopic conclusions. Unquestionably, highlighting the importance of pathworking is a thread that can be found through all of Dolores's impressive body of work, whether fiction, nonfiction, wonderfully whimsical children's books, or even the tarot decks she designed. To know oneself is the task, and the method to attain that knowledge is pathworking. The goal? Reflective yet again of another beautiful Gemini attribute, that of generosity, Dolores herself says, "Know in order to serve."

A Sampling of Gemini Occultists

GERALD GARDNER
founder of modern Wicca
(June 13, 1884)

KENNETH GRANT
ceremonial magician and writer
(May 23, 1924)

MARCIA MOORE
astrolger and yoga teacher
(May 22, 1928)

ALEX SANDERS
founder of Alexandrian Wicca
(June 6, 1926)

STARHAWK
Reclaiming founder and ecofeminism author
(June 17, 1951)

SHAKMAH WINDRRUM
ceremonial magician and mambo
(June 6, 1931)

THE SWAY OF YOUR MOON SIGN

Ivo Dominguez, Jr.

The Moon is the reservoir of your emotions, thoughts, and all your experiences. The Moon is your subconscious, your unconscious, and your instinctive response in the moment. The Moon is also the author, narrator, and the musical score in the ongoing movie in your mind that summarizes and mythologizes your story. The Moon is like a scrying mirror, a sacred well, that gives answers to the question of the meaning of your life. The style and the perspective of your Moon sign shapes your story, a story that starts as a reflection of your Sun sign's impetus. The remembrance of your life events is a condensed subjective story, and it is your Moon sign that summarizes and categorizes the data stream of your life.

In witchcraft, the Moon is our connection and guide to the physical and energetic tides in nature, the astral plane, and other realities. The Moon in the heavens as it moves through signs and phases also pulls and pushes on your aura. The Moon in your birth chart reveals the intrinsic qualities and patterns in your aura, which affects the form your magick takes. Your Sun sign may be the source of your essence and power, but your Moon sign shows how you use that power in your magick. This chapter describes the twelve possible arrangements of Moon signs with a Gemini Sun and what each combination yields.

Moon in Aries

Combine two quick-moving signs and you get a speedster. Your mind moves like lightning, and you are fast on your feet at work and play. You multitask better than most people and your idea of rest is exhausting for other people. You know a wide range of things and you are always learning more. You can get by on this most times, but to understand anything in depth, you need to make yourself slow down. Also, patience is a virtue that you need to acquire and foster as it is not a standard feature in this combination. That Aries Moon makes you more passionate and unfortunately also increases the ease at which irritation becomes anger. You are courageous, inventive, and often inspiring to other people. You have a strong drive to speak your truth regardless of the consequences. You like to juggle many things at once, but if you add one too many and they begin to fall, your stress can be extreme. Ask for help; you've built up a long list of favors owed to you for all you've done.

You are quirky and funny and know how to make friends and allies. You need to have enough friends and associates who jump at an outing or adventure. Although you love helping other people, you are equally good at taking care of yourself. You are not domestic nor domesticated, so your partners need to be energetic people with plans and goals of their own. Boredom or externally imposed limits make you chafe. Your thoughts are fast, and you are very perceptive, but that speedy flow also makes it harder to retain orderly memories. Note-taking, calendars, and recordings are your friend. Whenever possible, do not make on-the-fly decisions about important matters. You need time to recollect all the facts and details.

An Aries Moon, like all the fire element Moons, easily stretches forth to connect with the energy of other beings. The fiery qualities cleanse and protect your aura from picking up other people's emotional debris or being influenced by your environment. It is relatively easy for you to blend your energy with others and to separate cleanly. Your Gemini Sun uses this Moon's characteristics to extend the range of your psychism and your fluency in giving readings. This combination assists in interpreting dreams and visions.

Moon in Taurus

This fixed earth Moon is a tremendously useful complement to your changeable and volatile nature. You have all the wit and quickness of Gemini and the solid practicality of Taurus. You are a rock-solid friend, confidant, and ally. Never doubt that the ones who know you well love and respect who you are. You manage to retain a youthful and bright-eyed interest in life no matter what the years bring. Your Gemini Sun will lead to great adventures, both wonderful and troublesome, and your Taurus Moon will help you sift out what to keep and what is rubbish. Your personal magnetism will attract people to join you in your quests and chases. The good news is that most people will enjoy or benefit from being pulled along in your wake. This combination makes you a good judge of character, so even the best can't fool you for long. You'd do well in a leadership position or as a mediator.

That Taurus Moon also encourages you to turn your ideas into expressions that are lasting and tangible. This could mean creating poetry, art, architecture, a perennial garden, or almost anything else that others can experience. The Moon is said to be exalted in Taurus, which gives it greater power to add more serenity and centeredness to your personality. It makes you more determined to trek onward until your goals are reached. You love to be supportive, but be mindful that your support does not cross the line into being meddlesome. Listen to your own advice and imagine what it would be like to receive it. When you feel stuck, lean into being more a Gemini Sun and less a Taurus Moon.

A Taurus Moon, like all the earth element Moons, generates an aura that is magnetic and pulls energy inward. This Moon also makes it easier to create strong shields and wards. The auras of people with a Taurus Moon are excellent at holding or restoring a pattern or acting as a container or vessel in a working. You do well acting as a summoner or a vessel to attract spirits to you; you are the destination rather than the traveler to their realms. You have an aptitude for communicating with the Fae, nature spirits, and elementals. You also have a knack for fertility magick, plant magick, and attracting what you need.

♊

Moon in Gemini

A double dose of Gemini twins sets off a tornado of energy. That nervous energy keeps you moving even when you've run out of physical energy. This is great when you need to keep going and bad when you crash-land. Learn to listen to your body and tend it well so you can continue doing the things you love. Regular food and regular rest are needed. Yes, you may feel superhuman at times, but a lack of self-care can be your kryptonite. Routines may seem boring, but they will keep you at your peak. It is important to allocate your resources wisely because you love doing several things at once. You are brilliant, adaptable, and original, but time is a limited resource. If the cake recipe says to bake for an hour at a certain temperature, you can't have cake in thirty minutes by doubling the temperature. Physical activity and intellectual stimulation are the air you breathe; both are essential.

With this combination, the appearance and the personality you present to the world change fast. It is hard for people to keep up, so give them some clues about which part of you is running the show. You can go from tender to aloof or sweet to salty in moments as you respond to what you hear and see. Your sharp intellect does have the power to see from various perspectives and reconsider situations. You do have the power to manage who you become in response to the moment. Concentration, focus, and attention to detail do not come naturally, but you have what it takes to develop them. When you do, watch out world.

A Gemini Moon, like all the air Moons, makes it easier to engage in soul travel and psychism and gives the aura greater flexibility. When air aura reaches out and touches something, it can quickly read and copy the patterns it finds. A Gemini Moon gives the capacity to quickly adapt and respond to changing energy conditions in working magick or using the psychic senses. A wind can pick up and carry dust and debris, and the same is true for an aura. If you need to cleanse your energy, become as still as you can, and the debris will simply fall out of your aura. You are good at creating invocations, spells, and rituals.

Moon in Cancer

This Moon deepens your capacity to feel and identify emotions. You are more aware of your emotions and other people's feelings than most other Gemini. This Moon helps foster a good balance between head and heart, observation and imagination, and so on. The Moon rules Cancer, which gives it a stronger shaping influence on your psyche. Your memory is strong, especially when it comes to people and places. You also want more security and stability than is usual for a Gemini. You like to apply your creative flair and energy to make a calm and attractive home. So long as you are discerning in your choice of friends and associates, you can be very successful in life. You are good-hearted and have a tendency to give too much of yourself away to others. You have great adaptability, but that does not mean you have to fit in and conform.

You love being around people, but until you know someone well, you do not open up or share anything of consequence. You can be so charming that people don't realize you've been keeping them at a ten-foot distance until you let them come closer. It is probably better this way because once trust is broken or you are hurt, it is hard for you to move on. You are a great protector, so if someone you care about is harmed, you will do all you can to remedy the situation. You want to nurture the world. This may be through the arts or literature, through groups both informal and formal, by being a mentor or teacher, or by the deep power of friendship.

A Cancer Moon, like all the water Moons, gives the aura a magnetic pull that wants to merge with whatever is nearby. Imagine two drops of water growing closer until they barely touch and how they pull together to become one larger drop. The aura of a person with a Cancer Moon is more likely to retain the patterns and energies that it touches. This can be a good thing or a problem depending on what is absorbed. This matters even when doing solo work. The last spell or ritual you did can get stuck in your head like a song on repeat, so cleanse thoroughly. This combination usually comes with a gift for shape-shifting and stealth magick.

Moon in Leo

Fiery Leo excites and enlivens your Gemini air. You know you are a big deal and should get on with the big projects you have in mind. The challenge comes from having a dual nature that is one part trailblazing entrepreneur and one part happy-go-lucky comic. When these are well balanced, your enthusiasm will draw the people and situations you need to you. It is work that will feed your soul. When you are overwrought, this combination can lead to outbursts that can create a lot of drama. Is social media really your friend? Your lion comes out to roar, but it doesn't last for long. You may be over it, but give time for others to settle down. Your fun and positive side comes out to mend connections quickly. Pride; everyone needs the right amount, and you have more than your share, which can lead to conflicts that do last when you stop listening.

You are fiercely independent and see rules as suggestions to be followed when they suit you. When you explain the reasoning behind your choices and actions, there will be less friction. It is not immediately obvious because you can be so lighthearted, but you are profoundly loyal. This combination tends to be highly romantic and idealistic, typically about people, but for some, this energy is directed to arts and media more intensely. Those who are close to you need to be independent and self-sufficient because you do need breathing space to be yourself. When you are young, you may be restless and unsteady in picking a course and staying with it. Actively ask the universe for clues and guidance rather than using trial and error and educated guesses.

A Leo Moon, like all the fire element Moons, easily stretches forth to connect with the energy of other beings, though a little bit less than Aries and Sagittarius. The fiery qualities act to cleanse and protect your aura from picking up other people's emotional debris or being influenced by your environment. It is relatively easy for you to blend your energy with others and to separate cleanly. The Leo Moon also makes it easier for you to find your center and stay centered. Your magick is well suited to cleansings and healing others. You also can act as a catalyst that awakens magick in the people around you when you reach out your energy. You can also unintentionally awaken ghosts and memories that slumber in buildings or places.

Moon in Virgo

You get a second helping of Mercury's energy because Virgo is ruled by Mercury. Virgo is mutable energy, so you get a double dose of that as well. The earthiness of Virgo also makes you appear less like a Gemini. This blend makes you more detail focused and methodical and grounds your intuition in facts, which makes it more valuable. You do need to cultivate structured work habits to accomplish all you desire. You have an air of casual sophistication that tends to put most people at ease. The advice and help you give is very useful, but keep an eye on those who are on the receiving end of your words. Your very beneficial and accurate words may land like sharp criticism. You can use your command of language and your gut instincts to reframe or redirect their response so that it ends up being productive. You are invested in helping people live productive and healthy lives.

When you encounter a question or a mystery, your first instinct is to go digging for facts. This is especially true if you have less interesting tasks on your to-do list. You are a hard worker, but it can seem like you procrastinate because you don't always complete your list in order of priority. Guard against this as much as you can and be kind to yourself as you drag yourself back on track. Compassion for yourself is necessary for your physical and mental health. Health and healthy practices are important topics for you. Remind yourself of your dual nature as a Gemini and that health is about balance when that Virgo Moon demands perfection. Being human is not a sign of inadequacy. You are a good listener, so when a situation is unclear, slow down, collect more information, and think about the context and possible repercussions.

A Virgo Moon, like all the earth element Moons, generates an aura that is magnetic and pulls energy inward. This Moon also makes it easier to create strong thoughtforms and energy constructs. You have strong shields, but if breached, your shields tend to hang on to the pattern of injury; get some healing help, or the recovery may take longer than it should. Spells and workings related to oaths, promises, bindings, and agreements are assisted by this Moon. Healing magick for the health of the environment is also favored.

Moon in Libra

A Libra Moon encourages you to get along with others, to adapt to circumstances, and to use what you have been given. You are good at attracting powerful friends and allies because people can feel your optimism and love of harmony. Despite living in perplexing times, you can usually find a way to make it through and enjoy life. This grace does have a downside in that you sometimes walk away from opportunities that will be challenging and require some conflict. You can be a good mediator and a spokesperson for important causes and issues, but you must be willing to step into the turmoil. You love the power of fantasy and the imagination, and going inward can be a great resting place, but you will fade if you stay there. Your Gemini nature needs contact with people and places to remain vital and flourishing. The more you explore, the more alive you will feel.

Although you are caring and accommodating to your friends and partners, you will not tolerate being ignored, underappreciated, or put upon. Keep looking until you find the right people. Also, you find it difficult to tell whether someone is flirting with you. Ask direct questions; it will save time. You are tolerant and open-minded about most things so long as your happiness, and that of your beloveds, is not at risk. Pick which battles you'll take on and which are a waste of your well-chosen words. You are good at spotting trends in pop culture, society, business, and pretty much anything related to groups of people. This could be just fodder for conversation or part of your livelihood. You are inherently a member of many communities because you are a complex blend of identities. This can be a great benefit to you if used with awareness and finesse.

A Libra Moon, like all the air Moons, makes it easier to engage in soul travel and psychism and gives the aura greater flexibility. When you are working well with your Libra Moon, you can make yourself a neutral and clear channel for information from spirits and other entities. You are also able to tune in to unspoken requests when doing divinatory work. This Moon also helps you do work for sweetening sour situations, making peace, healing emotions, and encouraging personal development. Venus is Libra's ruling planet, so you also have a gift for the magick of love, beauty, and self-worth.

Moon in Scorpio

A Scorpio Moon pours a tremendous amount of emotion into your Gemini mind. As a Gemini, you are always alert and scanning your environment, and the Scorpio Moon makes you look deeper and sharper. You also have an amazing imagination that can serve you well or create drama when you imagine or enlarge or distort what you perceive. You also pick up on other people's emotions, which is a gift and a challenge. Unlike most Gemini, you tend to hang on to thoughts and feelings and play them on repeat in your mind. Practices to release these and to relax are important for your health and happiness.

The Scorpio Moon can give you more determination, and that means when you commit, you are all in. Like most Geminis, you seem easygoing, but when needed, you are unflinching and audacious.

When you take an interest in someone, you can be remarkably intense. Try to ramp up slowly so you don't scare people off. Also resist the urge to run when people say they have deep feelings for you. This Sun and Moon blend also makes it easier to notice the darkness and turbulence within yourself and in the world. You can swing between being overly proud and your own worst critic. The middle between these two is the personal truth you are looking for. You can stop the cycle by listening to your gut, thinking it through, and seeking the ear of someone you trust and admire. You are creative and enterprising, but some help on following through and sticking with your plans and deadlines is needed. Scorpio Moon gives you an air of mystery and enchantment. You do love your secrets, and other people love to give you their secrets; this is a sacred trust. How well you keep them is how well you will feel about yourself.

A Scorpio Moon, like all the water Moons, gives the aura a magnetic pull that wants to merge with whatever is nearby. You easily absorb information about other people, spirits, places, and so on. Your path for purification is to feel things fully so you can fully release them. Your words or thoughts can turn into magick when you are emotional, so be careful. You have a gift for sigil work and writing and performing incantations and invocations. Mediumship is an option for you, but you need to have spirit guides or human warders while you do the work.

Moon in Sagittarius

Your Sun is opposite to this Moon, and this air and fire combo can be overstimulating—though admittedly lots of fun. You are always on the go mentally or physically. You have enough interests to keep you busy for several lifetimes. You are a jack-of-all-trades and a master of some, though how many you master will be set by how much self-discipline you acquire. If something is romantic, otherworldly, foreign, or odd, it has your full interest. While that interest lasts, it will blaze bright in the center of your attention, and then it won't. You tend toward optimism and seeing the glass as half full. However, when things are truly a mess, you will tell your story as if it were an epic saga. Your love of being a free spirit and your revolutionary nature always lead you to explore the fringes. You know how to camouflage yourself to look normal, businesslike—whatever is needed to get in the door, but it is an act.

Your exuberance and inspiration often put you in the spotlight. Be attentive and thoughtful of what you say and what you say you'll do. Your reputation is often shaped by what you've said in a moment of passion. It is not always fun, but you do know how to work a crowd. You prefer candor and saying exactly what you mean without a filter. This will gain you accolades and trouble depending on the situation. When it doesn't work out, remember that you have humor and a silver-tongue on your side. In the end, even your adversaries are likely to admit you have admirable traits.

The auras of people with a Sagittarius Moon are the most adaptable of the fire Moons. Your energy can reach far and change its shape easily. You are particularly good at affecting other people's energy or the energy of a place. Like the other fire Moons, your aura is good at cleansing itself, but it is not automatic and requires your conscious choice. This is because the mutable fire of Sagittarius is changeable and can go from a small ember to a pillar of fire that reaches the sky. You may have a favorite type or style of witchcraft or magick, but you are a generalist at heart. You can fit into a wide range of traditions and rituals so well that you may be mistaken for being a member when you are a guest.

Moon in Capricorn

The swift mentality and curious nature of Gemini is given structure and direction by the cardinal earth of Capricorn. You will surprise people because you can be serious and driven but also witty and fun. You can go from free-associative creativity to step-by-step analysis with no effort at all. The Capricorn Moon may fool some folks into thinking you are more conventional than you really are. This Moon makes you more competitive, and your Gemini Sun is ambivalent about your need to succeed. It is not reasonable or possible to be good at everything, so don't feel bad when you aren't the best. It is praiseworthy that you have high standards and try to reach them. That really is enough. You have a strong sense of honor and dignity, and if you don't try to school the witless, you'll stay clear of spectacles that serve no purpose. There is something political in almost everything you say or do. By *political*, I mean your actions are intended to influence people's perspectives and actions. To some people, it may look like you are socializing, but you are always working to nudge the world in the direction you want.

Your communication skills and sense of purpose make you influential. You didn't have the easiest of childhoods. That is all the motivation you need to do what you can to make things better. Your principles and the people you trust will keep you grounded and connected to your hopes. Ego is an issue with this Sun and Moon combination. There is a tendency to think too highly of yourself, and then events bring about the reverse, and you think too little of yourself. Take stock of the facts and assess who you are and who you want to be so you can plan but not judge. You are affectionate and caring, but sometimes you need to schedule time so there will be opportunities to show it.

A Capricorn Moon, like all the earth element Moons, generates an aura that is magnetic and pulls energy inward. What you draw to yourself tends to stick and solidify, so be wary, especially when doing healing work or cleansings. The magick of a Capricorn Moon is excellent at imposing a pattern or creating a container in a working. Your spells and workings tend to be durable. You have a talent for protective magick, banishings, and curse-breaking. Time-walking—spiritual time travel—is something you may want to try.

≈≈

Moon in Aquarius

With both your Sun and Moon in air signs, you tend to lead with your head rather than your heart. Make no mistake, you are perceived as friendly and interesting, but you avoid letting your emotions get too intense. However, when you are talking about issues, causes, and interests, you come across as more passionate than when talking about people and personal matters. You are avant-garde and experimental. You don't see a need to follow norms unless you see a reason that appeals to you. This also extends to your sense of what friendships and relationships should be. To avoid unnecessary discomfort or heartbreak, be very clear and precise in sharing your thoughts so that everyone is on the same page. Loyalty and connection matter to you, but freedom and options have equal say in your choices.

This combination lets you see many different angles and perspectives at once, so you will often notice details and trends others miss. You might be just a step ahead in time than others. Make use of the opportunities that information creates. Knowing is good, but doing is better. To find your motivation to get involved and follow through on your goals requires that you look inward. You spend so much time observing others and your surroundings that you neglect examining yourself. Although you are tolerant and broad-minded as a general rule and sociable, you tend to only become close to people who share a good portion of your core values. It may not be the first thing that comes to mind for you, but relaxation and slowing down to enjoy life recharge you so you can do everything else. You have a harder time understanding other people's stronger emotions. When you are relaxed and unhurried, pay attention to other people to improve your reading of their emotions.

Like all the air Moons, the Aquarius Moon encourages a highly mobile and flexible aura. You have an air Moon, so grounding is important, but focusing on your core and center is more important. From that center, you can strengthen and stabilize your power. People with an Aquarius Moon are good at shaping and holding a specific thoughtform or energy pattern and transferring it to other people or into objects. You have skill in divination for groups, whether that be covens, businesses, nations, or circumstances that affect many. There is also a gift for enchanting objects.

Moon in Pisces

The twins of Gemini take a swim with Pisces' two fish, and the lines between what is in you and what is outside of you become fluid and blurred. You can be overwhelmed in waves of emotion coming from other people. You feel compassion and make every effort to offer kindness and consideration. This blend does give you great intuition, psychism, and the words and images to describe what you receive. However, this combination also makes it harder for you to maintain good boundaries. The more you learn about yourself, the easier it will be to draw the line between what is yours and what is not. This will not make you cold or cruel. It will make you more capable of helping yourself and others. Many of your doubts and bouts of indecision will lessen as you understand yourself and your aspirations. You will also become more authentic and let others know what you truly feel and think.

Your imagination and creativity will open the way for many career options. This doesn't necessarily mean you will be in the arts, but it does mean that your originality will be the key to success. For example, you can always come up with several ways to describe or explain something, which is useful in teaching, negotiating, and so on. You give off a welcoming air and have an endearing sense of humor and whimsy that will help both your work and your home life. Do be careful lest your imagination lead to fantasies that keep you from living in the here and now. The double dose of mutable energy means that unless you choose to keep grounded and anchored, you'll make poor choices based on impressions rather than facts.

With a Pisces Moon, the emphasis should be on learning to feel and control the rhythm of your energetic motion in your aura. Water Moon sign auras are flexible, cohesive, and magnetic, so they tend to ripple and rock like waves. Pisces Moon is the most likely to pick up and hang on to unwanted emotions or energies. Rippling your energy and bouncing things off the outer layers of your aura is a good defense. Be careful, develop good shielding practices, and make cleansing yourself and your home a regular practice. Practices that involve going into trance come easily for you, but make sure you have a helper. Your storytelling is a form of magick as well.

TAROT
CORRESPONDENCES
Ivo Dominguez, Jr.

♊

You can use the tarot cards in your work as a Gemini witch for more than divination. They can be used as focal points in meditations and trance to connect with the power of your sign or element or to understand it more fully. They are great on your altar as an anchor for the powers you are calling. You can use the Minor Arcana cards to tap into Jupiter, Mars, or Sun in Gemini energy even when they are in other signs in the heavens. If you take a picture of a card, shrink the image and print it out; you can fold it up and place it in spell bags or jars as an ingredient.

Gemini Major Arcana

The Lovers

All the Air Signs

The Ace of Swords

Gemini Minor Arcana

8 of Swords	Jupiter in Gemini
9 of Swords	Mars in Gemini
10 of Swords	Sun in Gemini

• MY MOST GEMINI WITCH MOMENT •

Laura Tempest Zakroff

As someone who is an artist, an author, a performer, a teacher, and an event organizer (among other things), I tend to have a lot of Gemini witch "moments" that are pretty out-there. These are times or things that seem normal to me at the time, but not really to everyone else who's watching the show. You mean other people don't wear six or eight metaphorical hats at once?

It's a frequent situation because I never can seem to do just one thing. Mix in my Cancer rising and Virgo Moon, and you've got the recipe for someone who loves to create and craft community while also having a hard time delegating authority because things have to be done a certain way. While I have definitely gotten better over the years, I often have overexhausted myself trying to do too much. I tend to forget that I'm just one person.

A case in point is one of the many festivals I've organized. Waking Persephone is an event I've been running since 2012.

As with all my events, I saw certain needs in my community that I felt drawn to address, and so I set about organizing a new event like a kite in a hurricane. From 2008 to 2010, I coproduced an event called Gothla US, which focused on celebrating dark/gothic fusion belly dance and related arts. The event was supposed to alternate coasts annually but ended up taking place each year in Southern California due to the other producers. At the time, I was living on the East Coast, which meant that most of my students and local community were unable to attend. It didn't make sense to me to put so much work into an event that few local to me could benefit from. I was also already handling so much for that event (the website, vendors, ritual events, registration, graphic design, etc.), I knew I could successfully produce my own events in my own backyard. So that's how Waking Persephone was born.

While the tagline for the event has changed over the years from "Dancing Through/Exploring the Dark and Unusual" to "A Celebration of the Queer and Magical," many of the goals have stayed the same. Those goals include featuring both established and up-and-coming voices, creating a home for us weird folks to feel comfortable, and offering a platform for new projects and ideas often rejected by other more traditional events. Waking Persephone has taken place in Providence, RI, Seattle, WA, and online during the pandemic. At different parts of its incarnation, it's spanned up to four days and nights and involved hundreds of people from all over the world—artists, dancers, musicians, poets, students, teachers, and the general public.

The first year I handled pretty much everything myself from start to finish. To begin with, that meant finding and booking a venue; posting a call for submissions from teachers and performers; hiring two live bands; creating and maintaining the website as well as the postcards, posters, merch, and other promo material; crafting the schedule and gala lineup; selecting and placing vendors; selling and tracking tickets to the event; and coordinating volunteers. I also hosted several performers at my own home and picked people up from the airport. In addition, I taught two workshops, had a solo performance with a band and another one with my students, led folks in community ritual to start off the event, and coordinated an after-dinner party. I did all of this producing while going through a divorce, working a full-time design job, and planning a cross-country move. I have probably left out about half a dozen other tasks that I managed to squeeze in there because that's just how I rolled back then.

I know now that it was unhealthy to take on so much, but at the time I couldn't see any other way to make it happen—especially with the vision I had in mind. Of course I had to do all the things—how else would it happen?! That's when the magic kicked in to manifest the event, and with approximately six months to pull it all off, I got to work. Creating something out of nothing is really one of the things I do best. When I take on things like this, I don't ask, "Will this happen?" but rather focus on *how* it's going to happen. In order not to feel too overwhelmed about producing such a big event, I focused on one or two tasks at a time. Each part was a puzzle piece, and I would jump around as I got stumped about how something would work out. Eventually when I did come back to a problem, I often had a new way of seeing a solution. Each step wove the event together a little more. Up went the posters and ads in the local papers, postings on social media were shared, questions were answered, schedules were coordinated, and lineups were crafted.

Finally, it was time for the event. People were arriving! I organized and directed the space, I welcomed folks in ritual, I taught, I performed, I vended, I emceed, and I put out fires. I herded a motherload of cats. I didn't eat or sleep much while the event was happening, but I managed to make it happen and live through it. Thankfully other folks got caught up in the whirlwind of the moment and also stepped in when they could to help. In the end, the first event was a hit and folks begged me to do it again—as I was falling asleep into my post-event dinner! And while some may question my sanity, I agreed that it should happen again.

Luckily, those folks also recognized all the work I was doing and stepped up to help out in advance, which made the successive events easier as I learned to delegate authority and handed out tasks. I appointed someone else to coordinate the volunteers, another to handle the vendors, another person to sort out housing and rides for visiting performers, and so on. Each one removed one task from my plate and put it on competent shoulders. Which was still scary as hell when I'd been used to doing everything and worried it was not going to get done right. But I had to remind myself, just because my sign is multiple people, doesn't mean I can split myself in two (or more).

There's another duality that's very much in the Gemini wheelhouse. When it comes to producing an event, there are essentially two major moments: all the time planning the event in advance, and then the event as it's going down. You can plan all you want in careful, calculated detail (which you should!), but there's always going to be a surprise or challenge you didn't see coming. You get better at anticipating potential issues with each successive event. But there's *always* something unexpected to deal with. Flight delays, traffic, temporarily lost instruments, massive bad weather systems, sickness, last-minute cancellations, vendors who don't read emails, dancers who didn't prepare their music properly or who bring a fire hazard onstage, sound system issues, venues partially under construction that was supposed to be wrapped up weeks ago, leaving nails and debris on floors where movement classes will take place—any and all of these things can and have happened. The trick is to keep cool and pull into the energy of the moment. Because once an event in underway, it's essentially a juggernaut. The event takes on a life of its own, and you've got to ride along with it regardless. You're riding the dragon and you've got see this thing through, which brings a mixture of both exhilaration and peaceful resolution.

It's been over ten years now since that first Waking Persephone marathon, and I've slowed down in many ways. Which isn't a bad thing—it's actually a very good thing! I've learned not to pile as much on my plate, how to collaborate with other like-minded folks to shoulder the tasks and craft events together, and to honor my own health, emotional and mental well-being, and boundaries. In turn, I think the events I do are better in many ways *and* I get to enjoy them a bit more. I can still get in a little over my head, but it's much more manageable. The thing is, I love creating these experiences for others. I love to see so many beautiful, diverse, engaging people gathered together in one spot. I love creating opportunities for others to share what they do best—be it their art, a dance, a song, a story, or some other talent. I revel in providing a place for education that's hard to find anywhere else. I strive to make my events as accessible as possible, be it ability or budget—a definite challenge, but so important and necessary to recognize. I enjoy creating spaces that are opportunities for others to network, share, and find other like-minded beings.

The trick, I have learned, is finding a balance in how I mentally, emotionally, and physically approach events. Sure, I can make some amazing stuff happen out of virtually nothing, but the work needs to be sustainable for not only the community, but for my own well-being as well for the whole journey of the event from start to finish.

Both Sides of the Coin: Seeing the Whole Truth Spell

Christopher Allaun

Sometimes we Geminis get a bad rap. People who don't know the Gemini personality see us change from one point of view to another, always changing our minds on a whim. The twined zodiac is often called "two-faced" because some seem to think we cannot make up our minds or at worst do not have conviction in our judgments. This is far from the truth. The beauty of the Gemini mind is that we have an amazing ability to see "both sides of the coin." Whenever two people disagree, we instinctively take a step back and try to see both points of view. It is often said that there is your point of view, my point of view, and the truth. So, we Geminis try our best to see the truth in its entirety.

Do you ever get that feeling that you are only being told part of the truth? Or there's something someone is not telling you? For this spell, we will conjure the energies of Gemini so we may see the whole truth. To do this spell, you must place yourself in a state of mind that is ready for the whole truth. We must temporarily suspend our judgments and preconceived notions about the subject and be ready to receive the whole truth, no matter what it is. This spell may manifest immediately or may take several days. The truth always comes when you are ready to hear it.

You will need:

- A large handheld mirror or reflective surface (a sheet of aluminum foil will work in a pinch)
- Two white candles
- Blue lace agate
- Quartz crystal
- Two quarters
- Peppermint and lavender, dried or fresh

Instructions:

Place your mirror, reflective surface, or aluminum foil on your altar or sacred space. The purpose of this is to reflect the information back to you. Place each white candle about four inches apart in the center of your reflective surface. Each candle represents the two different sides of the truth.

Now, place the blue lace agate and the quartz crystal between the two candles. Blue lace agate summons the energies of communication while quartz amplifies these energies.

Place one quarter faceup next to the left candle and place the second quarter facedown next to the right candle. The quarters will help your consciousness connect to each point of view of the truth. Take a small handful of both the lavender and the peppermint in your hand and think of the truth.

Allow yourself to be open to all possibilities, even if the truth is hard to hear. Place these herbs in a ring around the candles.

Light the candles and visualize yourself surrounded by the white light of truth. Again, be open to the truth in whatever form it chooses to manifest for you. Now, holding the visualization, say aloud, "I see the two sides of the same coin. I understand the truth in its wholeness. As these candles illuminate the dark, so does the truth illuminate my mind."

Once the candles are burned out, you may place them in a sachet or mojo bag to use as a talisman to summon the truth.

YOUR RISING SIGN'S INFLUENCE

Ivo Dominguez, Jr.

The rising sign, also known as the ascendant, is the sign that was rising on the eastern horizon at the time and place of your birth. In the birth chart, it is on the left side on the horizontal line that divides the upper and lower halves of the chart. Your rising sign is also the cusp of your first house. It is often said that the rising sign is the mask you wear to the world, but it is much more than that. It is also the portal through which you experience the world. The sign of your ascendant colors and filters those experiences. Additionally, when people first meet you, they meet your rising sign. This means they interact with you based on their perception of that sign rather than your Sun sign. This in turn has an impact on you and how you view yourself. As they get to know you over time, they'll meet you as your Sun sign. Your ascendant is like the colorful clouds that hide the Sun at dawn, and as the Sun continues to rise, it is revealed.

The rising sign also has an influence on your physical appearance as well as your style of dress. To some degree, your voice, mannerisms, facial expressions, stance, and gait are also swayed by the sign of your ascendant. The building blocks of your public persona come from your rising sign. How you arrange those building blocks is guided by your Sun sign, but your Sun sign must work with what it has been given. For witches, the rising sign shows some of the qualities and foundations for the magickal personality you can construct. The magickal personality is much more than simply shifting into the right headspace, collecting ritual gear, lighting candles, and so on. The magickal persona is a construct that is developed through your magickal and spiritual practices to serve as an interface between different parts of the self. The magickal persona, also known as the magickal personality, can also act as a container or boundary so that the mundane and the magickal parts of a person's life can each have its own space. Your rising also gives clues about which magickal techniques will come naturally to you.

This chapter describes the twelve possible arrangements of rising signs with a Gemini Sun and what each combination produces. There are 144 possible kinds of Gemini when you take into consideration the Moon signs and rising signs. You may wish to reread the chapter on your Moon sign after reading about your rising sign so you can better understand these influences when they are merged.

Aries Rising

It is possible that a Gemini with an Aries rising was the template for creating Peter Pan. Your desire to do everything and go everywhere is sped up and stimulated by the Aries rising. You never lose the ability to get excited, enthused, and passionate the way a teenager can. You love being playful and a hint of competition makes everything more interesting. Your reactions are often loud and visible, so people notice you. Because of this, you often become the center of attention. Most people with this combination benefit from physical practices that are well structured and become a routine. It doesn't matter whether it is yoga, tai chi, dance—so long as you do it. This burns off excess energy so you can concentrate and reduces your nervous energy.

Having the ruling planets of Mercury and Mars active in your chart means you will exude power, poise, and mischief. Be advised that not everyone understands your verbal sparring and physical humor are meant as harmless fun or sometimes flirting. You'll do better if you read the room and adjust how you present. Adjust your inner settings to the age and maturity level that fit the circumstances. People want to like you, and you can recruit allies easily, and they'll let it slide when you misfire, but don't push your luck. You can bring out the best in others when you bring out the best in yourself. Like all of us, your drive and resolve will wax and wane, but never doubt that they will always return.

An Aries rising means that when you reach out to draw in power, both air and fire will answer easily. If you need other types of energy, you need to reach farther, focus harder, and be more specific in your request. This combination often attracts the attention of the Fae, so take care. You excel at spells for strength, confidence, or removing obstacles. These can be cast for yourself or others.

Taurus Rising

The earthy solidity of this rising gives your Gemini nature more stability, pragmatism, and restraint than most. The Taurus rising focuses and sorts the myriad of interests and impulses you have so you can complete them fully and well. You also are more likely to slow down enough to smell the roses and enjoy all the sensual delights of life. Your mind is still as quick and analytical as that of any Gemini, but the Taurus rising makes it more likely that you will not blurt out your first idea. You will speak when you have run through the possibilities and are ready to stick with your statement. You don't like arguments or conflict and if there is too much noise and emotional turmoil you become distracted or obstinate. It is better that you leave until things cool down rather than becoming more embroiled.

Venus rules Taurus and, combined with Mercury for Gemini, encourages you to be trustworthy, circumspect, and frugal. This combination asks your Gemini energy to behave in ways that yield longer-lasting results. This rising encourages you to look at your values and your sense of harmony to make choices that nourish your life. Rising signs change how you perceive things, and, combined with your Gemini Sun, this combo allows you to see creative ways to reuse, revamp, and renovate whatever you have before you. You hate to see waste.

Taurus rising gives more strength in your aura and the capacity to maintain a more solid shape to your energy. This gives you stronger shields and allows you to create thoughtforms and spells that are longer lasting. This combination also makes you a better channel for other people's energy in group work because you can tolerate larger volumes of different types of energies. You can act as an amplifier to boost individuals or small groups to increase their magickal or psychic abilities.

♊

Gemini Rising

Double the Gemini magnifies all the classic traits of your sign. You are always looking for new experiences, fresh conversation, new music, and styles that express your mood. You like to be on the cutting edge, to be an early adopter, an explorer of where the next big change is coming. You move easily between different age-groups, backgrounds, cultures, and so on. You can be quite the chameleon without too much effort. Learn to breathe deep and listen more than you speak. You'll miss out on less when you do so. You tend to have many acquaintances and few true friends. The problem is that your open and interesting personality gives people the impression they are your friends when they are just acquaintances. Communicate more carefully to reduce the hurt feelings.

Generally, you are a positive person, but if you are blocked from communicating your ideas for too long, your frustration may turn into anger and actions vented at whoever is nearest. If your feelings of being obstructed persist long enough, you go past anger and into an unfeeling determination to get what you want. You may roll over or push people aside and regret your actions when you are back to yourself. Before you get this blocked up, backtrack, make new plans, use that amazing imagination to find a way around the situation. Ask for help; you'll get all you need.

This rising helps your energy and aura stretch farther and adapt to whatever it touches. This combination can lend itself to communication with animals, plants, crystals, and anything with a spirit. You can pick up too much information and it can be overwhelming. Learn to close and control your awareness of other people's thoughts and feelings. You have a gift that can help or hinder technology and can impact the digital realm.

Cancer Rising

Cancer rising makes you a bit more reserved when meeting someone new, but you open up quickly if they are sincere. Like most Geminis, you are observant and communicate well, but the Cancer rising gives you more insight into emotions and motivations. You can often describe what a person is feeling or wanting better than they can. This sensitivity can be brought to bear in work as a teacher, counselor, translator, negotiator, and so on. There are many other ways you can use this skill. However, some may be unnerved by your sensitivity, and you may pick up on their discomfort and misinterpret it. Try to remain neutral and don't jump to conclusions about how others feel about you. More often than not, it is about the situation and not about you.

Cancer rising means you enjoy being at home more than the average Gemini. You still do your sharing of exploring, but you need a home base. Cancer also gives you a love of the past and history and a touch of sentimentality. There is also a pull to be more nurturing and preserve living beings and material goods that have emotional value and memories attached to them. You tend to be drawn more to the generations before or after yours. Gemini Sun wants to accelerate quickly into any activity. Listen to your Cancer rising and warm up and start slow before going full speed. Do this, and you will avoid errors and irritation.

Cancer rising grants the power to use your emotions, or the emotional energy of others, to power your witchcraft. Though you can draw on a wide range of energies to fuel your magick, raising power through emotion is the simplest method. This rising produces ease and power in Moon magick of any sort. You are also good at charging oils, waters, and other liquids. You may have a calling for dreamwork or past-life recall.

Leo Rising

Leo is ruled by the Sun and lights up your airy Gemini skies to give you a sunny and lively disposition. You manage to be interested in or appreciate almost everything you find around you. You are good at getting people to talk and are completely in your element when you lead discussions or debates. You are articulate and can come up with the right language to catch hearts and minds. You aim for compassion and honorable behavior in all areas of your life. Don't promise yourself or others that you will get so many things done. Your enthusiasm often exceeds the amount of energy you have available. Leo is firmer in its stance than Gemini, which can help you complete the goals you have set for yourself. The downside is that, when thwarted, Leo rising mixed with those Gemini winds can get very stormy.

This blend has charisma that can fill the room. With your communication skills and your magnetic charm, you can be very influential and convincing in expounding on your perspectives. Even if you are not officially in charge, you are in a leadership role because of your personality. You are fearless in most situations, except when you find out that you made an error or had the wrong information. The more you learn to let go of the agitation this provokes, the smoother your life will be.

Leo rising means that when you reach out to draw in power, fire will answer first. If you need other types of energy, you need to reach farther, focus harder, and be more specific in your request. Your aura and energy are brighter and steadier than most people's, so you attract the attention of spirits, deities, and so on. Your Sun and rising give you an aptitude for energy healing. You also can control the emotional and spiritual atmosphere of a room with ease.

Virgo Rising

Virgo and Gemini are both ruled by Mercury, so its influence is doubled. Gemini's capacity to collect all the information and Virgo's attention to detail and careful analysis can be wonderful or frightful. You are an organizational whirlwind sweeping through the world. You are sharp and incisive in your understanding of most matters. However, be careful when you use your sharp tongue and apply a detailed takedown on someone. You easily underestimate the impact of your words and opinions. You have a strong calling to be of service, to work for a healthier world. In your eagerness, you may neglect getting enough rest and recreation. You may be drawn to journalism, content creation, teaching, or anything where you can reach large numbers of people.

You are shyer and pickier than most Gemini when it comes to friends and partners. You have the Gemini skill of conversation and social interaction, so opening your mind is easy. It has to be someone special to open your heart and keep it open. Mental hygiene is important for you; please make use of meditation, discussion groups, or therapists. It's not the years, it's the mileages, and you are always zooming down that mental highway.

Virgo rising with a Gemini Sun makes it easier to work with goddesses and gods who are connected to the element of air, wisdom, communication, and healing. You are good at spells and rituals to let go of patterns and habits that do not serve you. You are a good diagnostician who can figure out what is wrong with a ritual, what is preventing a healthy flow of energy in a person or home, and so on. Be careful when you entwine your energy with someone else because you can pick up and retain their patterns and issues. Always cleanse your energy after doing solo or collective work.

Libra Rising

This combo has double the air and a mix of compatible planets with Libra's ruler being Venus and Gemini's being Mercury. When you step into the room, everything tries to harmonize with you. There is something in your aura that is like a fragrance, music, or a familiar feeling that makes people open up to you and be inclined to like you. Use your power to fascinate others with kindness. You have a strong interest in harmony, aesthetics, and beauty. For you, these are connected to your spirituality and your witchcraft. These interests may also lead to careers or vocations. Be honest with yourself about preferring to be a rolling stone than a cornerstone. Talent is not a question in the plans you undertake; the question is whether you'll have the desire to stay with them.

You will be tugged at, texted, emailed, called, cajoled, and expected to give up some of your time and attention by many people. For your sake and the sake of the people you actually want to spend time with, say no more often, redraw, and reinforce your boundaries. Don't forget to read the fine print in written agreements, the subtext in conversations, and pay attention to your intuition. Your Libra rising wants you to be fair and treat everyone equally; this is not true for some people. Your Gemini Sun knows it is necessary to save the best parts for yourself and your beloveds.

When you expand your aura, your personal energy can settle down an unruly or unwholesome atmosphere or calm down irritated spirits. Magick related to bringing peace or justice is favored by this combination. Rituals or spells to mend friendships and relationships or improve communication are favored. This combination also works well in creating crystal grids, working altars, magickal gardens, or other physical instances of beauty and magick.

Scorpio Rising

You scrutinize, you dig, and you dispel illusions with your piercing intellect. When you want something or to know something, you'll find a way to get what you need. Think twice, count to ten before you say it, ask what impact your words will have, then say what you must. The Scorpio rising gives you powerful emotions and even stronger willpower. When risky, and sometimes dangerous, situations present themselves, you walk right in. If there is a dark place within yourself, others, the world, or the other worlds, you want to know it and understand it. Your thought process is complicated, layered, and woven through with many strands of emotion. Though you are creative, you tend more toward investigation, research, or specialties that make the most of your probing mind.

To love and to be loved in return is a goal you hold in secret. You radiate sensuality, which can be a problem or a gift. This rising is cautious about sharing their deep self, so humor, snark, and hot takes will be used to hold others at arm's length. Remind yourself that we all make mistakes, and choose forgiveness when it is possible and reasonable. Sometimes, the best option is time and distance. Scorpio rising can make you more reactive to drugs, toxins, and allergens, so be careful. That said, you have significant regenerative powers and can overcome most physical ills.

Scorpio rising makes your energy capable of pushing through most energetic barriers. You can dissolve illusion or bring down wards or shields and see through to the truth. You may have an aptitude for breaking curses and lifting oppressive spiritual atmospheres. It is important that you do regular cleansing work for yourself. You are likely to end up doing messy work and you do not have a non-stick aura. You are a natural in rituals or workings to explore past lives, call the dead, or reveal hidden truths.

♐ Sagittarius Rising

Your Sagittarius rising is the opposite of your Gemini Sun, which creates a vigorous polarity. When in balance, it brings out the best traits in both signs. Sagittarius loves understanding, the big picture, optimism, and ambitious plans that support the broad searching interests of a Gemini Sun. This blend of fire and air with Sagittarius ruler Jupiter being added to the mix allows you to see opportunities and options others would miss. You value direct speech, which means your bluntness can get you into predicaments, but you often smooth things over with your positive intentions. You are constantly looking to improve yourself and you know that progress usually follows a wiggly line. Your criticism of yourself and others tends to be constructive rather than destructive.

Sagittarius loves freedom and expressing their opinions. Gemini loves freedom to explore and communicating about almost anything. It is easy to see the good situations and the dilemmas that arise from this combination. Let joy and positivity guide you as these are always in you. Thankfully, over time, you learn to navigate the complexities of expectations, social settings, cultural patterns, and political differences to become a great ambassador for whatever cause or idea you care about.

Sagittarius rising adds mutable fire to your mutable air so your aura changes shape at will. Talent in the use of candles, wands, or staves is favored by this combination. This is because you can push your energy and intentions into objects with ease. You have a talent for rituals and spells that call forth creativity, wisdom, and freedom. You attract the attention of spirits and divine beings easily. You can be a voice for them if you wish. This combination gives access to lots of energy, but you can fry yourself with the intensity of the current. Make it your practice to stop and cool off and then start again.

Capricorn Rising

Your rising sign and your Sun are starkly different, which creates an inner tension that never quite resolves. This friction can give you determination and ambition. It makes you concentrate more on work and accomplishments, which take the wide span of your Gemini consciousness and focus it laser sharp. When people first meet you, it may be some time until they see your Gemini nature. You are not as sociable, are more serious, and are more forceful. You tend to be harder on yourself than other people. Since you are goal oriented, remind yourself that you can't do better unless you see your own progress and potential.

You hold on to hurt feelings from the past, and this can cloud your perception of the present.

You have a deep need for a core group of people in your life. This can't happen unless you take chances. Yes, you'll get hurt and you'll recover. Trust in your strength to grow and change. You'll also collect casual friends and associates on this journey who will help you reach other goals. Your creativity and originality become more practical when guided by your Capricorn rising. You present and act in a more adult fashion than many Geminis. You are more decisive as well. You handle your money and work life with great attention to detail.

Capricorn rising creates an aura and energy field that are slow to come up to speed, but have amazing momentum once fully activated. Make it your habit to do some sort of energy work or meditative warm-up before engaging in witchcraft. Try working with crystals, stones, and even geographic features like mountains as your magick blends well with them. Your rituals and spells benefit from having a structure and a plan of action. Spells for removing obstacles, clear thinking, and business ventures are favored.

♒

Aquarius Rising

This rising brings a second dose of the element of air, which puts an emphasis on thought and the powers of the mind more so than communication. Some may say you have fire in the head, but really it is electricity. You buzz with an energy that others notice. For the most part, you are humanitarian and have a dozen plans, perspectives, and ideologies to make the world better. You like collective work and being on a team in theory, but you can find it hard to compromise. To make your ideas real, you must meet reality in the middle. Your offbeat humor and eccentric views will help you find a way.

You may have interest in developing or improving systems of transportation, distribution, mass media, or communication. You often think in terms of the impact ideas or technology will have on populations. Your mental life is rich and interesting. Sometimes it is too interesting, and you forget to follow through on what you've promised individuals. Caring about people arises from a mental and rational connection first that may, with time, become

an emotional connection as well. You are affectionate but rarely clingy. Those close to you need to be
equally innovative or grounded and bighearted. Be
watchful of what you put into yourself, whether it
be ideas or substances. Your nervous system is high-
strung and needs no additional strains upon it.

Aquarius rising helps make it easier for you to
consciously change the shape and density of your
aura. This makes you a generalist who can adapt
to many styles and forms of magick. Witchcraft
focused on calling inspiration, creating community,
and personal transformation are supported by this
combination. Aquarius rising is gifted at turning
ideas into reality. Mind magick, psychism, weather
magick, and energy work are good options for you.

Pisces Rising

This rising brings in more mutability, flowing emotions, and psychic perceptions. Most of the time,
you are sensitive, tender, caring, and aware of others' needs. You are good at seeing the best in people
or things and knowing what small changes would

transform good to superb. Unfortunately, it is hard to examine yourself and apply the same refinements. As such, you can suffer from bouts of self-doubt. Look to the people who are dependable and good-hearted in your life so they can give you good counsel. Many people hold you in high regard, and you need to let them tell you how they see you.

You love to change the look of your clothing, hair, and home. People look forward to seeing what you've done and if they'd like to try it. Geminis can have trouble staying on track, and a Pisces rising makes it easier for you to get distracted. If you don't adopt a habit of keeping deadlines and keeping track of progress on your tasks, you'll disappoint yourself and others. It is necessary for you to do wide-ranging searches and trial runs to find the jobs, friends, and partners that best match who you are. Part of your criteria for your ideal circumstances must include settings and people who help ground you and keep you on track.

Pisces rising with your Gemini Sun opens the gates of the imagination, the dreamworld, and the upperworld. You have a distinctive gift for helping others find their way to other levels of reality. You can do astral travel, hedge riding, and soul travel in all their forms with some training and practice. You have a gift for interpreting and understanding old magick and updating it so it can be used now. Music, poetry, chanting, and dance also provide fuel for your witchcraft.

A DISH FIT FOR A GEMINI: CHOOSE YOUR OWN ADVENTURE BURRITO BOWLS

Dawn Aurora Hunt

* * *

Since Gemini love a good adventure and trying new experiences, this recipe is perfect because it will give ideas and inspirations for flavor combinations and easy meal prep, along with strong, bright, and enticing colors and flavors.

Options create opportunity. Making a large spread of different ingredients that can be worked into endless tapestries of flavor, color, and energy keeps things interesting and fun for you, Gemini. The following inspiration for burrito bowls is not only filled with spiritually energetic ingredients that will keep your palate interested, but each bowl can help with multiple goals. For example, if you are trying to increase passion in a relationship, load up your bowl with peppers for passion and shrimp for romance. Or top your chicken with grilled pineapple and roasted corn to invite the energy of the Sun into your life. In some cases, Geminis might get overwhelmed with choices and need to focus more clearly; in this case, accompany this meal with a beverage containing a small amount of caffeine, like iced tea, which will sharpen awareness.

Note: If your diet precludes you from eating meat or shrimp, experiment with other tasty ingredients like sweet potatoes, cauliflower, and jackfruit marinated and sautéed using the spice rub and olive oil.

Ingredients:

+ 2 cups cooked white basmati rice
+ Chopped cilantro or parsley
+ Juice from 2 limes
+ Salt
+ 2 pounds uncooked shrimp, tail on
+ 2 pounds chicken breast, cut into chunks
+ 12 ounces fresh pineapple chunks
+ 3 red bell peppers, sliced
+ 1 red onion, sliced
+ 2 poblano peppers, sliced
+ 1 tablespoon olive oil

Spice Rub Ingredients:

+ 1 teaspoon salt
+ 1 teaspoon pepper
+ 1 tablespoon granulated onion
+ 1 tablespoon granulated garlic
+ 1 tablespoon paprika
+ 1 tablespoon sugar

Other Ingredients/Inspirations:

+ 1 cup cherry tomatoes, cut in half
+ 1 jalapeño pepper, minced
+ 1 cup shredded sharp cheddar cheese
+ 1 cup frozen roasted corn kernels, thawed
+ 1 cup canned black beans, drained

Directions:

Make the spice rub by combining the six ingredients in a small container and stirring until combined. Set aside.

Prep your proteins. Using grill-safe skewers, skewer at least five pieces of chicken per skewer and five shrimp per skewer, using separate skewers for chicken and shrimp. Place them on a long pan, continuing until all the protein has been threaded onto the skewers. Sprinkle them all with spice rub and brush them with olive oil or spray them with cooking spray. Set aside.

Prep your pineapple. Using grill-safe skewers, fill skewers with pineapple chunks and set aside.

In a large skillet, heat one tablespoon of olive oil. Sauté bell peppers, onions, and poblanos until just tender. Sprinkle with salt and pepper and remove to a covered dish until ready to serve.

Heat a gas grill or grill pan on the stove to high heat. Working in batches, grill each of the skewers. Grill the chicken for about three to five minutes on each side until the chicken is cooked through. Grill the shrimp skewers for about two minutes or less on each side, just until the shrimp has turned pink. Grill the pineapple just until char marks form on each side—about three minutes. Remove each item from the grill and place in its own dish.

Put freshly cooked rice in a large serving bowl and toss it with the juice of two limes, chopped cilantro or parsley, and salt to taste.

Lay out all the ingredients in separate bowls and create your own flavor combinations!

RECHARGING AND SELF-CARE

Laura Tempest Zakroff

In this section, we'll look at a few healthy ways to support your Gemini energy. Self-care may seem like a buzzword lately, but please don't fall into the trap of dismissing this work as superfluous or simply trendy. Having routines that support wellness are essential to being a witch. When we don't take time to recharge and address our needs, we can become irritable, disorganized, and anxious. This makes us feel disconnected from our magic and others.

3 Rules to Thrive By

To give you a sense of how important self-care is, I'm going to share with you the three rules we live by in our household:

1. Take care of yourself.
2. Take care of others.
3. Don't be a jerk.

Self-care most obviously falls under Rule #1, but it's underscored by the others. If you're not taking care of yourself, it's extremely hard to take care of anyone else. And when you're not taking care of yourself or the people you care about, it's very easy to be a jerk.

Dealing with Stress

To begin to understand how to incorporate self-care into your practice, consider what stresses and limitations you deal with on a subconscious level daily. Whether others have imposed these boxes upon us or we have grown up believing this is how others will like us, they're common obstacles to real self-care. Release yourself from certain expectations you feel others may have of you:

- You don't have to do all of the things.
- You don't have to have or give an opinion on everything.
- You don't have to know everything.

That's a lot of weight to carry around emotionally and mentally. Stress may be "invisible," but it has very real effects on our minds, bodies, and spirits. If you're feeling anxious, having problems sleeping, getting frequent headaches, respiratory issues, and/or recurring skin problems—these are all common stress symptoms for Geminis. As you work to release those expectations, consider these ideas instead:

- You can accept help from others.
- You can let go of things that no longer interest you.
- You can take the time you need.

To help work these ideas through your body, do the following:

1. Take a deep breath in for a count of three seconds, centering your focus on your heart and lungs as your chest expands. Exhale for three seconds. Repeat two more times.

2. Now focus on your shoulders—flex them forward and back a bit, then shrug them up and push them down a couple of times. As they begin to feel more loose, roll them forward and back and around as you feel comfortable. Then relax.

3. Next, turn your head from side to side, then point your chin up and then down. Repeat until you feel comfortable softly rolling your head clockwise and counterclockwise.

4. Check back in with your shoulders and then take one more deep breath in and exhale out. You should now feel more engaged yet relaxed in your upper body.

Stimulating the Learning Self and Quieting the Mind

I find that I have two major modes as a Gemini witch. There's the part of me that's excited by new things, experiences, and adventures. Then there's the part of me that craves familiarity and doesn't want to be stimulated or encounter anything unknown. Both can be effective approaches for self-care practices.

Geminis do not fare well with monotony. Going through the same motions day in and day out can be quite draining if we're not getting enough mental stimulation to keep us engaged. We like to be challenged, we enjoy learning, we love opportunities to flex our mental muscles and chances to be creative. Otherwise, we start to lose interest—often feeling underutilized or unappreciated. This condition is true not only for work situations, but also for romantic relationships, too. Of course, most of us can't just quit our jobs when we feel bored. We also know that relationships take collective work to be successful, which means we have a hand in making changes. The key is learning how to recharge properly and knowing when it's a good time to take a break.

True to your innate dualistic nature, there tends to be two contrasting approaches when it comes to recharging your Gemini self. Depending on the situation, we either need a full-on immersion experience or we need to withdraw completely and shut everything off. Technically, when you think about it, they're both the same sort of approach, yet two very different energetic experiences—a recharge and a reset, respectfully.

Immersion

An immersion experience is an opportunity to shake things up. It can be a new learning opportunity, such as a new course of study, a day trip to an unfamiliar place, or trying an activity that's new to you like scuba diving or basket-weaving. It doesn't have to be something long and drawn out like a six-week cruise or a new educational degree, but rather a short jaunt or class that excites our brains and our senses. A change of scenery works wonders for our sense of self, and we're thrilled to come back with something new to talk about. Whether we do the immersion with someone else or not depends a lot on the activity and who's coming along with us. We tend to like sharing experiences with groups of folks we're comfortable with, but we can also get easily frustrated if folks draw us out of the experience in some way. However, if someone's not on the same page with us, doesn't match our enthusiasm, or just prefers to complain or antagonize, we're going to have a harder time recharging. That's why it's important that if you need company for whatever excursion you choose, they're a good match and meet you at least halfway. Even better if they're more adventurous than you!

Here's a list of ideas for immersive recharging:

+ Take a hands-on or skill-oriented class or work-shop.
+ Look to the arts—seek out live music, a theatrical presentation, a poetry or storytelling slam, a gallery night, or an art festival.
+ Try joining a social club or outing group that interests you, especially where you don't have to do the planning and all you need to do is show up.
+ Get involved in a game night, trivia challenge, or other fun competitive or collaborative group effort.
+ Listen to podcasts, deep-dive on topics that fascinate you, discover new bands, watch something you might not normally check out.

Going Dark

Now, at the other end of the spectrum is essentially what some call "going dark." This means taking a break from social media, disconnecting from groups and large gatherings, and generally just being quiet and contemplative. Alone time is crucial for recharging. We could really make the joke that Geminis have two modes: "talking" and "off." This would clearly be engaging our "off" button. But there's a bit more nuance to powering down than simply shutting ourselves off. We're likely not going to want to sit in a dark room in the corner to recharge. Instead, what works for quieting our minds may look nonrestful to others. Here are some examples:

- Going out into nature or getting a major change of scenery. We are deeply influenced by our environments, and shaking things up often does us a world of good. Whether it's going for a walk around the block or taking a hike, engaging our physical bodies and being more passive about what's in front of us is very healing. It's also a lot harder to look at your phone or computer when you're out in the wilderness and can't plug in. The same is true for gardening—as you're going to get your hands dirty and the plants will likely require your full attention.

- Other kinds of exercise that fascinate both the mind and body, such as dancing, martial arts, fencing, or horseback riding. While all these activities require us to be mentally present, they tend to be more relaxing while our bodies are stimulated. However, activities that don't have enough mental stimulation to keep us present tend to be draining.

- Engaging in low-anxiety/low-investment media. Rather than watching a new program or movie all the time, Geminis often like to turn to familiar favorites as a sense of comfort. We already know what's going to happen, so we don't have to pay a whole lot of attention, but we still enjoy what's happening. The same is true for watching what I tend to call "big dumb shows." Every Gemini I know has a few of these proverbial skeletons in their closets. Whether it's a racy reality show, a sappy holiday special, or lowbrow comedy that we'd be abhorred to admit to watching to others, they provide us with entertainment that just lets our brains rest. Along this same vein is playing video games. They can be a great way to slip into an alternative reality and explore stories without too much stress (depending on the game, of course).

♦ Cleaning and bathing practices that cleanse the mind. Two of the simplest things I can do to reset myself both involve cleaning: taking a bath and tidying my home. Physical cleaning is especially helpful when we can't pinpoint or immediately influence the source of our stress because we still feel like we're doing *something*. When we take a ritualistic bath, we can create a rich environment that smells and feels good, and even relax with a good book! A few candles, some bubble bath, and a good tincture mix can really make a difference.

As for cleaning your home, it takes a lot more work, but we're essentially tapping into the same kind of routine that exercise provides us with. My recommendation is to keep it small, though; do a little at a time. I often suggest that most folks start with the bathroom sink and toilet area as they're often pretty easy to clean but make a quick visual difference.

+ Art as meditation. In the stimulation section above, I listed some active/social arts-based activities. Art as meditation is often a more solitary or antisocial activity—and you'll probably appreciate the alone time even more. Painting, drawing, playing an instrument, weaving, journaling, knitting, and other crafty activities can put you into a trancelike and meditative state. Your brain settles into the task at hand while your body leads the process. You can also mix a little magical intention into the task, too!

These are all just suggestions you may find helpful. You know your body and mind best. So, the next time you're feeling a bit out of sorts, ask yourself which approach might get you back on track: stimulating or quieting the mind? Then get to it!

Polishing the Diamond: A Ritual Bath for the Gemini Witch

Austin Nix

The internal world of a Gemini can be a tricky space to navigate. Anyone with a basic grasp of astrology could assume what the Gemini mind is like: energetic, ever changing, fractal. We are far from immune to our own mercurial nature, however.

Geminis can easily find themselves caught at a crossroads of our own making—forced to marry the many disparate parts of our lives and personalities to find a sense of harmony. Consider Atu VI of the tarot, more commonly titled The Lovers, which is assigned to Gemini. This tarot trump represents the pathway between an inner nucleus of harmony and the gates of mystical union, through which flows the understanding that without *Solve* there is no *Coagula*.

As such, the most useful practice you could choose is one to dissolve the cacophony of your mental world into one focused stream of thought. It is easy to become overextended in the "jack-of-all-trades, wearer of many hats" spirit, but it is vital (especially as a practitioner of magick!) to implement a regular practice of softening such duality into singular awareness. As Geminis, we possess a diamond mind, and although its multifaceted quality is a source of inherent beauty, like all precious gems, it must be polished to maintain its clarity.

Water can be an effective element to counteract a Gemini's airy nature, and there is no better way to still the flighty Mercury-mind than with self-care.

You will need:

+ Bath salts or bubble bath (optional)
+ Candles (optional)
+ Incense

Instructions:

Set yourself up a nice bath, including any materials you prefer, like bath salts, bubbles, oils, or candles. Use magickal correspondence if you will, but focus intently on creating a calming space for your body and mind. Light a stick of incense (sandalwood if you're unsure) and make yourself comfortable in the water.

Close your eyes and visualize a large diamond suspended in space, cloudy and covered in smudges. Spend a few moments watching the diamond rotate slowly and take notice of any haziness that might dim its natural glimmer.

Turn your attention to your breath. Begin counting the seconds on each inhale and exhale, ensuring that they are full and of equal length. Find a natural space in the pauses. When you exhale, imagine that the diamond begins to spin faster, becoming less cloudy each revolution. Continue until the diamond is in its natural state of perfect clarity, revolving and refracting so clearly that you can hardly see the divisions of its facets.

This exercise should take no more than twenty to thirty minutes. When your bath is done, visualize your disco ball diamond coming gently to rest in a black velvet box for safekeeping until its next polishing.

DON'T BLAME IT ON YOUR SUN SIGN

Laura Tempest Zakroff

How many times have you heard someone say, "Oh that's because you're a Gemini," or express something similar about their own sign? While your Sun sign can be a handy reference and guide for a lot of traits and behaviors, nothing's set in stone. Stereotypes do tend to have a kernel of truth to them, but that doesn't mean they're telling the whole story. It can be far too easy to blame your Sun sign for almost anything. When the Sun sign is used as an excuse to avoid responsibility or addressing issues, it can reinforce limitations and fears. In this section, we'll look at some traps related to the sign of Gemini and how to best navigate them.

Flights of Fancy and Focus

Geminis are often described as flighty, flakey, unfocused, capricious, and as having short attention spans. That we have too many interests and not enough substance. (Clearly this rumor was started by someone who wasn't a Gemini.)

In actuality, we're highly focused, but often on multiple aspects all at once, which can confuse and confound others. Observing and exploring numerous points of view means we need to be flexible and move around to do our research. So, it's really just a different type of focus and approach. However, if we're not interested or stimulated by what's presented, we will just move on. The trick is effectively communicating that to others who might not understand what the issue is. As a Gemini witch, I believe words have power, and it's important to remember to use them, especially when it may not be clear to others what we're thinking or doing. This also means following through with what we say when possible. If we're no longer interested or need more time to consider something, it's best that we express that versus not showing up or being ambiguous. Speaking our intentions aloud to others can also help solidify them in our own minds and hearts.

As for having "too many" interests and not enough depth, I'm sure you've heard the expression "jack-of-all-trades, master of none"—and even have had it thrown in your face as an insult. But the joke's on them. The full phrase is "a jack-of-all-trades is a master of none, but oftentimes better than a master of one." Knowing a fair amount of information about a lot of topics or being relatively skilled in multiple areas plays to Gemini strengths. We actively use what we know, even across platforms, styles, and cultures. Rather than being purists or singularly focused about one thing, we notice

similarities, blend compatible ideas, and use our cross-knowl-
edge to problem-solve rather effectively. The challenge is to
do enough studying or skill-developing so that your understanding is thorough instead of shallow or limited.

Remember to give yourself sufficient time to immerse
yourself in a subject before proclaiming yourself as an expert
of that topic. Being a jack-of-all-trades does not mean also
being an insufferable know-it-all. For example, when it comes
to being a Gemini witch—you don't have to be an expert on
herbalism, astrology, oils, tarot, runes, bones, crystals, tinctures, sigils, candlemaking, and a dozen other things. Sure,
some of these things are related, but there's no witch bingo
card you must fill up to be a "real witch." Take time to explore
the areas that interest you the most and hone your skills.
You will find it's also helpful to be friends with folks who are
experts in areas you are not. You don't have to know all the
things yourself, but it sure is handy to know who to go to
when you have a question!

Overthinking Overload

Sometimes our overthinking brains can get the better of us,
especially when we're amped up. Our imaginations can really
run away with us, causing unnecessary stress.

I remember quite a few years ago when I was giving a
talk about my second book, *Sigil Witchery*. This event was my
first time out doing author signings and chatting about the

book. It was in my home city at the time, but at a New Age shop I've never presented at before. Every shop has its own feel and market, so there were a lot of faces I wasn't familiar with in attendance. So I was a bit nervous to begin with.

But let me give you a bit of backstory before I continue. For my first book, I had organized an extensive countrywide tour, so by the end of the tour, I was *really* good at talking about that book. I had it down. The thing is, that sort of familiarity only comes out of experience. The kind that develops after presenting the same material in front of different audiences and figuring out what works and what doesn't. The trick is, every book is unique, so you start from scratch every single time. However, I didn't fully realize this until, of course, I had to go through it all over again with every book after.

So here I am on this little stage with my new book in front of about twenty people I didn't know. In walks a new friend from our local occult meetup group—I was elated to see a familiar face, but also now another layer of nervous because this group tends to be quite knowledgeable and nerdy. And here I am presenting my own unique take on a topic, quite aware of some of the edgelord attitudes that can plague the occult world when it comes to non-male voices. When I get nervous and am in the spotlight, words just seem to start spilling out of my mouth. Not just any words, but I can get more sarcastic and dramatic as well about things I feel deeply about. Most folks find it entertaining and fun, but I can be a real asshole if I'm not careful, even though I really don't want to hurt anyone's feelings. I'm about three-quarters of the way through my presentation when the friend gets up and leaves quietly. Now folks have to use the bathroom all the time, or have some other need to take care of, so they'll leave the room, but he doesn't come back. By the end of the presentation, I'm fixated on the fact that he left and clearly I said something to offend him. I was too brazen and loose with my words! I fret, I worry aloud to my partner, and I wonder how to make it right. I toss and turn all night worrying and am very angry with myself for getting carried away. I wake up all set to apologize for whatever it was I said when I see there's a message from him. He wrote that he's so sorry he had to leave early as he was really enjoying the talk, but he had to catch a bus to get back home. He bought the book on the way out, and could I sign it at the next meeting?

All that stress and worry because my overthinking brain perceived a situation that didn't actually exist. Another time when my overthinking nearly got the better of me was when I was traveling for an event, and we had a cat sitter staying with our kitties. This particular sitter is a mature older woman who is hit-or-miss with texts. You'll either get a lot of messages in a stream or nothing for a couple of days. That's just how it is, and we know she takes great care of the cats, so I tend to forgot that sometimes she's just hard to reach.

I got a message wishing us a safe journey when we left, but then didn't hear anything the next day and a half. I had sent a text about some package arriving but didn't hear anything. I began to worry and started to imagine that something had gone horribly wrong. What if she had fallen? What if she was hurt? *What if* ad nauseum. I called and left a message, trying not to sound stressed. I then reached out to a friend to see if they could stop by after work to check in on the cat sitter, since they had a key. They could indeed swing on by if I hadn't heard anything by the time they left work. I can't even think straight—I'm worried about the sitter, the cats, something happening to the house, and so on. Not even three minutes after arranging for the visit, the sitter texted that all was well. I had stressed myself out for at least four hours for nothing. On the upside, I could probably now write a horror movie script to sell to Netflix called *The Missing Cat Sitter*.

The moral of both these stories is, while my intuition is normally spot-on for many things, if I'm already in a stressful situation—whether it's being nervous or exhausted from traveling—I should really just shelve my brain until I'm in a better place. Because not only is the signal getting garbled and magnified by my own issues, it's usually completely off target.

The best thing you can do when you feel an overthinking stress spiral coming on is to focus on fact and proven knowledge—what you know and see for sure. Don't succumb to theories and what-ifs. Find a pleasant distraction, eat or drink something, take a nap; basically, reset your brain and your body. You'll be much better off and happier for it.

Oops I Overshared Again

Related to the story above is the tendency to overshare or basically word vomit all over others. Geminis have a reputation for being gossipers when really we're just obsessed with information and can accidentally cross lines we didn't even realize were there. When we're nervous or feeling emboldened, it can be really hard to know when to shut up. Oversharing has typically two consequences: we can overwhelm and/or upset others and/or we can feel major remorse when we realize too late that we've said too much or the wrong thing.

- Is this your story to tell?
- Is this the right audience for what you need to say?
- Are you in a confidential setting if you're sharing sensitive information?
- Are you about to say anything you know will bite you in the ass down the road?
- When's the last time you've taken a breath and checked in with your listening audience?

These may seem like really obvious things, but let's face it: we Geminis definitely could use a reminder from time to time.

Gemini Communication Charm

This short little rhyming charm is a good way to set the tone when you know you're about to do a lot of talking about something important:

> *May the words I speak come from the heart.*
> *May they unite and not set apart.*
> *May they be received as I intend.*
> *Off into the world, these words I send!*

POSTCARD FROM A GEMINI WITCH

Crystal Blanton

We Geminis think deeply, but we also FEEL just as deeply, if not more so. We hold both sides of the coin, the two balancing parts of the self; we Geminis are often an overload of both. In my developing knowledge about myself, I have come to understand the complexity of this balance instead of just experiencing sheer confusion. The amount of time I have spent in my life trying to reconcile what I feel with what I am thinking, and vice versa, would otherwise earn me a college degree.

The power of the Gemini has always been about balance for me. It is the knowingness that I cannot think myself into a magic existence, but I can harness a wealth of power through embracing the delicate balance.

In learning more and more about how to hold this energy in ways that support my goals, I have leaned heavily on the understanding of the Wise Mind concept within Dialectical Behavioral Therapy (DBT). Psychologist Marsha M. Linehan created the concept of DBT and identified the Wise Mind as a balance or integration of the emotional mind and the analytical or reasonable mind. While the emotional mind reacts from a place of emotion and feeling, the analytical mind reacts from a place of rational thought and "facts." The Wise Mind is the integration of both.

Supporting positive patterns that reinforce the Wise Mind hasn't just supported me in one area of my life but in all areas, including within my Gemini witchiness. Wise Mind is the goal, even within my spiritual workings and in my ability to manifest what I want, feel, and need as a part of living my path.

So, what does this mean for me in my daily unfolding of witchiness? Well, it means identifying what side of the balance I am leaning toward, being mindful of whether I am thinking or feeling too much to make a balanced decision or action, and utilizing Wise Mind tools prior to moving forward with any level of working. It means I am committed to a higher level of mindful and emotional awareness to minimize unintended consequences for all around me and not reacting when I am stuck within one side of the duality of my nature.

It also gives me permission to stop and tell myself, "Gurl, you better stop trippin' before you call in the ancestors." A very important message indeed.

• SPIRIT OF GEMINI GUIDANCE RITUAL •

Ivo Dominguez, Jr.

The signs are more than useful constructs in astrology or categories for describing temperaments; they are also powerful and complicated spiritual entities. So, what is meant when we say a sign is a spirit? I often describe the signs of the zodiac as the twelve forms of human wisdom and folly. The signs are twelve styles of human consciousness, which also means the signs are well-developed group minds and egregores. Think on the myriad of people over thousands of years who have poured energy into the constructs of the signs through intentional visualization and study. Moreover, the lived experience of each person as one of the signs is deposited into the group minds and egregores of their sign. Every Gemini who has ever lived or is living contributes to the spirit of Gemini.

The signs have a composite nature that allows them to exist in many forms on multiple planes of reality at once. In addition to the human contribution to their existence, the spirits of the signs are made from inputs from all living beings in our world, whether they are made of dense matter or of spiritual substances. These vast and ancient thoughtforms that became group minds and then egregores are also vessels that can be used by divine beings to communicate with humans. The spirits of the signs can manifest themselves as small as a sprite or larger than the Earth. The shape and the magnitude of the spirit of Gemini emerging before you will depend on who you are and how and why you call upon them.

There are many good ways to be a witch and a multitude of well-developed approaches to performing rituals. The ritual described in this chapter may or may not match your accustomed style, but for your first attempt, I encourage you to try it as it is written. Once you've experienced it, then you'll see which parts, if any, you wish to adjust to be a better fit for you. I'll give some suggestions on how to do so at the end of this chapter.

Purpose and Use

This ritual will make it possible to commune with the spirit of Gemini. The form the spirit will take will be different each time you perform the ritual. What appears will be determined by what you are looking for and your state of mind and soul. The process for preparing yourself for the ritual will do you good as well. Aligning yourself with the source and core of your energy is a useful practice in and of itself. Exploring your circumstances, motivations, and intentions is a valuable experience whether or not you are performing this ritual.

If you have a practical problem you are trying to solve or an obstacle that must be overcome, the spirit of Gemini may have useful advice. If you are trying to better understand who you are and what you are striving to accomplish, then the spirit of Gemini can be your mentor. Should you have a need to recharge yourself or flush out stale energy, you can use this ritual to reconnect with a strong clear current of power that is compatible with your core. This energy can be used for magickal empowerment, physical vitality, or healing, or redirected for spell work. If you are charging objects or magickal implements with Gemini energy, this ritual can be used for this purpose as well.

Timing for the Ritual

The prevailing astrological conditions have an impact on how you experience a ritual, the type and amount of power available, and the outcomes of the work. If you decide you want to go deeper in your studies of astrology, you'll find many simple or elaborate techniques to either pick the best day and time or to adjust your ritual to work with what fits your schedule. Thankfully, the ritual to meet the spirit of your sign does not require exact timing or perfect astrological conditions. This ritual depends on your inner connection to your Sun sign, so it is not as reliant on the external celestial conditions as some other rituals. Each of us has worlds within ourselves, which include inner landscapes and inner skies. Your birth chart, and the sky that it depicts, burns brightest within you. Although not required, you can improve the effectiveness of this ritual if you use any of the following simple guidelines for favorable times:

- When the Moon or the Sun is in Gemini.
- When Mercury is in Gemini.

- On Wednesday, the day of Mercury, and even better at dawn.
- When Mercury is in Virgo, where it is exalted.

Materials and Setup

The following is a description of the physical objects that will make it easier to perform this ritual. Don't worry if you don't have all of them as, in a pinch, you need no props. However, the physical objects will help anchor the energy and your mental focus.

You will need:
- A printout of your birth chart
- A table to serve as an altar
- A chair if you want to sit during the ritual
- A small dish or tray with feathers to represent the element of air
- An assortment of items for the altar that correspond to Gemini or Mercury (for example, a citrine, a carrot or lemon, and lavender flowers)
- A pad and a pen or chalk and a small blackboard, or something else you can use to draw a glyph

Before beginning the ritual, you may wish to copy the ritual invocations onto paper or bookmark this chapter and bring the book into the ritual. I find that the process of writing out the invocation, whether handwritten or typed, helps forge a better connection with the words and their meaning. If possible, put the altar table in the center of your space, and if not, then as close to due east as you can manage. Place the dish with feathers on the altar and hold your hand over it. Send sparks of energy from your hand to the feathers. Put the printout of your birth chart on the altar to one side of the feathers and arrange the items you have selected to anchor the Gemini and Mercury energy around them. To the other side of the feathers, place the pad and pen. Make sure you turn off your phone, close the door, close the curtains, or do whatever else is needed to prevent distractions.

Ritual to Meet the Spirit of Your Sign

You may stand or be seated; whichever is the most comfortable for you. Begin by focusing on your breathing. When you pay attention to the process of breathing, you become more aware of your body, the flow of your life energy, and the balance between conscious and unconscious actions. After you have done so for about a minute, it is time to shift into fourfold breathing. This consists of four phases: inhaling, lungs full, exhaling, and lungs empty. You count to keep time so that each of the four phases is of equal duration. Try a count of four or five in your first efforts. Depending on your lungs and how fast you count, you will need to adjust the number higher or lower. When you hold your breath, hold it with your belly muscles, not your throat. When you hold your breath in fourfold breathing, your throat should feel relaxed. Be gentle and careful with yourself if you have asthma, high blood pressure, are late in pregnancy, or have any other condition that may have an impact on your breathing and blood pressure. In general, if there are difficulties, they arise during the lungs' full or empty phases because of holding them by clenching the throat or compressing the lungs. The empty and the full lungs should be held by the position of the diaphragm, and the air passages left open. After one to three minutes of fourfold breathing, you can return to your normal breathing pattern.

Now, close your eyes and move your center of consciousness down into the middle of your chest. Proceed with grounding and centering, dropping and opening, shifting into the alpha state, or whatever practice you use to reach the state of mind that supports ritual work. Then gaze deeply inside yourself and find yourself sitting on the ground in a garden. Look at the beauty of the crystal and the plant materials. Take a breath and smell fresh air and refreshing fragrances. Pick up a feather and gently move the air and awaken all the places and spaces within you that are of Gemini. When you feel ready, open your eyes.

Zodiac Casting

If you are seated, stand if you are able and face the east. Slowly read this invocation aloud, putting some energy into your words. As you read, slowly turn counterclockwise so that you come full circle when you reach the last line. Another option is to hold your hand over your head and trace the counterclockwise circle of the zodiac with your finger.

> *I call forth the twelve to join me in this rite.*
> *I call forth Aries and the power of courage.*
> *I call forth Taurus and the power of stability.*
> *I call forth Gemini and the power of versatility.*
> *I call forth Cancer and the power of protection.*
> *I call forth Leo and the power of the will.*
> *I call forth Virgo and the power of discernment.*
> *I call forth Libra and the power of harmony.*
> *I call forth Scorpio and the power of renewal.*
> *I call forth Sagittarius and the power of vision.*
> *I call forth Capricorn and the power of responsibility.*
> *I call forth Aquarius and the power of innovation.*
> *I call forth Pisces and the power of compassion.*
> *The power of the twelve is here.*
> *Blessed be!*

Take a few deep breaths and shift your gaze to each of the items on the altar. Become aware of the changes in the atmosphere around you and the presence of the twelve signs.

Altar Work

Pick up the printout of your birth chart and look at your chart. Touch each of the twelve houses with your finger and push energy into them. You are energizing and awakening your birth chart to act as a focal point of power on the altar. Put your chart back on the altar when it feels ready to you. Then take the pad and pen and write the glyph for Gemini again and again. The glyphs can be different sizes, they can overlap; you can make any pattern with them you like so long as you pour energy into the ink as you write. Scribing the glyph is an action that helps draw the interest of the spirit of Gemini. Periodically look at the items on the altar as you continue scribing the glyph. When you feel sensations in your body, such as electric tingles, warmth, shivers, or something that you associate with the approach of a spirit, it is time to move on to the next step. If these are new experiences for you, just follow your instincts. Put away the pen and paper and pick up the sheet with the invocation of Gemini.

Invoking Gemini

Before beginning to read this invocation, get in touch with your feelings. Think on what you hope to accomplish in this ritual and why it matters to you. Then speak these lines slowly and with conviction.

> *Gemini, hear me, for I am born of the wind's*
> *mutable air.*
> *Gemini, see me, for the Gemini Sun shines*
> *upon me.*
> *Gemini, know me as a member of your*
> *family and your company.*
> *Gemini, know me as your student and your*
> *protégé.*
> *Gemini, know me as a conduit for your*
> *power.*
> *Gemini, know me as a wielder of your*
> *magick.*
> *I am of you, and you are of me.*
> *I am of you, and you are of me.*
> *I am of you, and you are of me.*
> *Gemini is here within and without.*
> *Blessed be!*

Your Requests

Close your eyes and look within for several deep breaths, and silently or aloud welcome the spirit of Gemini. Close your eyes and ask for any guidance that would be beneficial for you and listen. It may take some time before anything comes through, so be patient. I find it valuable to receive guidance before making a request so that I can refine or modify intentions and outcomes. Consider the meaning of whatever impressions or guidance you received and reaffirm your intentions and desired outcomes for this ritual.

It is more effective to use multiple modes of communication to make your request. Speak silently or aloud the words that describe your need and how it could be solved. Visualize the same message but without the words and project the images on your mind's screen. Then put all your attention on your feelings and your bodily sensations that have been stirred up by contemplating your appeal to the spirit of Gemini. Once again wait and use all your physical and psychic senses to perceive what is given. At this point in the ritual, if there are objects to be charged, touch them or focus your gaze on them.

Offer Gratitude

You may be certain or uncertain about the success of the ritual or the time frame for the outcomes to become clear. Regardless of that, it is a good practice to offer thanks and gratitude to the spirit of Gemini for being present. Also, thank yourself for doing your part of the work. The state of heart and mind that comes with thanks and gratitude makes it easier for the work to become manifest. Thanks and gratitude also act as a buffer against the unintended consequences that can be put into motion by rituals.

Release the Ritual

If you are seated, stand if you are able and face the east. Slowly turn clockwise until you come full circle while repeating the following or something similar.

> *Return, return oh turning wheel to your*
> *starry home.*
> *Farewell, farewell oh nimble Gemini until we*
> *speak again.*

Another option while saying these words is to hold your hand over your head and trace a clockwise circle of the zodiac with your finger. When you are done, look at your chart on the altar and say,

It is done. It is done. It is done.

Afterward

I encourage you to write down your thoughts and observations of what you experienced in the ritual. Do this while it is still fresh in mind before the details begin to blur. The information will become more useful over time as you work more with the spirit of Gemini. It will also let you evaluate the outcomes of your workings and improve your process in future workings. This note-taking or journaling will also help you dial in any changes or refinements to this ritual for future use. Contingent upon the guidance you received or the outcomes you desire, you may want to add reminders to your calendar.

More Options

These are some modifications to this ritual you may wish to try:

+ Put together or purchase Gemini incense to burn during the ritual. A Gemini oil to anoint the feathers or yourself is another possibility.

* Set up a richer and deeper altar. In addition to adding more objects that resonate to the energy of Gemini or Mercury, consecrate each object before the ritual. You may also want to place an altar cloth on the table that brings to mind Gemini, Mercury, or the element of air.

* Creating a sigil to concentrate the essence of what you are working toward would be a good addition to the altar.

* Consider adding chanting, free-form toning, or movement to raise energy for the altar work and/or for invoking Gemini.

* If you feel inspired, you can write your own invocations for calling the zodiac and/or invoking Gemini. This is a great way to deepen your understanding of the signs and to personalize your ritual.

Rituals have greater personal meaning and effectiveness when you personalize them and make them your own.

GEMINI ANOINTING OIL RECIPE

* * *

Ivo Dominguez, Jr.

This oil is used for charging and consecrating candles, crystals, and other objects you use in your practice. This oil makes it easier for an object to be imbued with Gemini energy. It also primes and tunes the objects so your will and power as a Gemini witch flow more easily into it. Do not apply the oil to your skin unless you have done an allergy test first.

Ingredients:

- ✦ Carrier oil—1 ounce
- ✦ Lavender—5 drops
- ✦ Lemongrass—4 drops
- ✦ Tea tree—2 drops
- ✦ Peppermint—6 drops
- ✦ Cardamom—2 drops

Pour one ounce of a carrier oil into a small bottle or vial. The preferred carrier oils are almond oil or fractionated coconut oil. Other carrier oils can be used. If you use olive oil, the blend will have a shorter shelf life. Ideally use essential oils, but fragrance oils can be used as substitutes. Add the drops of the essential oils into the carrier. Once they are all added, cap the bottle tightly, and shake the bottle several times. Hold the bottle in your hands, take a breath, and pour energy into the oil. Visualize light yellow energy or repeat the word *Gemini* or raise energy in your preferred manner. Continue doing so until the oil feels warm, seems to glow, or you sense it is charged.

Label the bottle and store the oil in a cool, dark place. Consider keeping a little bit of each previous batch of oil to add to the new batch. This helps build the strength and continuity of the energy and intentions you have placed in the oil. Over time, that link makes your oils more powerful.

• BETTER EVERY DAY: THE WAY FORWARD •

Laura Tempest Zakroff

I hope you've come to realize that being a Gemini witch is more than just a label or something on your periphery of being. It's part of who you are and how you interact with the world around you. An essential part of developing an authentic practice is fully embracing who you are and tapping into your natural abilities and powers. To help you succeed in building that practice, this section includes ideas, exercises, and suggestions to really "Gem" it up!

A Little a Day

Daily practice doesn't have to be complicated or extensive. I always recommend that folks start with looking at what they're already doing every single day. What are the little rituals that make up your day-to-day life? From your first cup of morning brew to showering, taking care of animals, and getting dressed—these are all excellent opportunities to add a little magic. Even better, you can find ways of easily

incorporating some of the other activities we discussed earlier. Here are some ideas to help you fully immerse yourself
in the stream of Gemini energy:

- Anoint yourself with a special oil after bathing.
  I like to dab a little on one wrist and rub my other
  wrist against it to spread the oil to both points.
  I then take a moment to take in the scent of the
  oil changing as it makes contact with my skin.
  Go one step further mentally as you perform this
  anointing by recognizing your left and right wrists
  as the twin aspects of yourselves coming together.

- Read a small passage from a book of wisdom for
  a few minutes each day. You probably have an
  impressive TBR (to be read) stack just waiting
  to be cracked open. If you select a book that has
  numerous short sections (such as a book on herbs,
  crystals, or divination), you can practice a little
  bibliomancy and fascinate your mind at the same
  time!

- Practice daily affirmations. As Geminis, we sure
  can talk and charm a whole lot—but that's usually with other people. Our inner monologues
  often venture into negative territory, which can be
  unhealthy. We can balance the inner critic with an
  inner fan by repeating some short positive sayings

to ourselves. You can say the words aloud to your reflection in a mirror or work them into a meditation. Some examples: *I am proud of who I am. I embrace my quirks as my strengths. I am not "too much." I bring creative change. I share my knowledge with love.*

• Use adornment as magic. I have certain pieces I always put on when I'm about to leave the house—a particular necklace and at least two evil eye bracelets. These are part of my daily protections. Everything else I put on after that adds another layer of meaning and magic. It's not just about matching an outfit, but rather seeing what feels good to wear and what helps me tap into the part of my personality I want to utilize that day. You can extend this to clothes, makeup, shoes, bags, hats— whatever helps strengthen how you wish to feel and appear to others.

These are just a few pointers to incorporate more Gemini witch magic into your daily life. Don't be afraid to experiment and embellish—and most importantly, have a bit of fun while you're doing it!

Working the Gemini Sigil with the Body

A long time ago, when I was working on coming up with a personal sigil for myself, I landed on a combination of a pentagram (five-pointed star) placed in the center of the sign for Gemini. The star then appears to be holding up the glyph or emerging from the doorway between the two pillars. The pentagram for me symbolizes the intersection of earth, air, water, fire, and spirit, as well as the human body itself. If you squint your eyes a bit, the star takes on the character of Leonardo da Vinci's "Vitruvian Man"—the upward-pointing top is the head, the side points are the arms, and the bottom points are the legs.

My witchery is centered around recognizing the body as my most powerful and immediate magical tool—and it's yours as well! We are spirit interwoven with flesh, learning to experience the physical world. We are physically composed of all of the elements, and each is present within us energetically. But it can be easy to forget this truth when we're distracted by the words of the world and lots of shiny things. This sigil serves as a reminder to not always exist in one's head, but also to spread the wealth to the rest of the body so we can experience life more fully.

In Ivo's Ritual to Meet the Spirit of Your Sign, you are instructed to draw the glyph for Gemini as part of the rite. While you can certainly follow the same approach with the Gemini sigil, for this exercise I'm going to lead you in drawing the sigil *with* and *through* your body. The goal is to get you to be more fully present in your body and ready to tap into that Gemini energy whenever you need it. Your body is the star, and the world around you becomes the Gemini glyph that frames you.

When first trying this exercise, don't rush through it. Work through it slowly, and be mindful of how your body feels at each step. Most importantly, listen to your body, and don't do anything that feels uncomfortable or hurts. Adjust as necessary or inspired. Start by standing with your feet a little wider than shoulder width apart and your arms relaxed at your sides. (If you're unable to stand, sitting with legs apart will work, too.) You are going to become the star within the glyph. If it helps you visualize better, you can stand in a doorway to get a very physical representation of the Gemini symbol. If it's a narrow doorway, you'll want to stand a little in front of it so you won't smack into it with your hands. If the doorframe is close to or a bit wider than your arm span, then you can stand in the middle of it.

1. Take a deep breath and let it out over the count of three seconds. Take a second deep breath, then exhale for a count of six seconds. Then take a third deep breath, and slowly let it out for a space of nine seconds.

2. To start to be more present in your body, begin by focusing on your feet. Rock your weight so that you shift from toes to balls to heels and back, slowly and gently. (If

you're seated, then flex at your ankles to roll your feet against the floor in the same manner.) Envision the floor as the base of the glyph being present under your feet.

3. Next, bring your focus up from your feet to your ankles and calves, slowly shifting, squeezing, and releasing the muscles in your calves. Gently bend and straighten your knees without locking them. Think of this motion as fluid and rolling, like the rising tide of the ocean moving up your body. Continue your awareness up to your thighs, hips, and belly, so that there's a sense of standing waist-deep in water.

4. Move your focus up to your chest, where your heart and lungs reside. Bring your hands up in front of your sternum. Take a deep breath in and expand and open your arms out from your chest as you exhale. Your arms should now be open and out, your hands reaching out to either side, palms facing in front of you. Depending on your body and level of comfort, your hands can be as high as your shoulders

or midway between your shoulders and hips. As you extend out, your arms will reach out to the "pillars" of the glyph on either side of you.

5. Now shift your attention from your chest and arms up through the center of your neck to your head. Think of the top part of the star and imagine the "ceiling" of the Gemini glyph above you and connect with it mentally (or look up to see it if you're standing in a doorway, if you have any problems visualizing).

6. Recall the "floor" of the glyph below and recognize your body is now the star in the middle. As above, so below. You should feel a sense of connection from the top of your head all the way down to your feet. At this point, you can summon energy from the glyph from all around you (up from your feet, in through your hands, down through your head). You can pull that energy into the center of your body like a ball of light, as well as push it back out to "illuminate" the glyph, the light

of your star. A simple way to consider this movement is to draw energy inward to stimulate your Gemini presence, or release it outward to send energy to others or relax your body.

Once you've got the feeling of connection down, this exercise is something you can do daily for a minute or two. This embodied sigil can be helpful as part of a morning balancing routine, to get you and your mind in motion. Or you can use it at the end of the day before you go to bed to calm your mind and prepare to rest. You can also utilize the Gemini sigil during ritual or as you're initiating spell work to get in the right frame (and body) of mind.

CONCLUSION

Ivo Dominguez, Jr.

no doubt, you are putting what you discovered in this book to use in your witchcraft. You may have a desire to learn more about how astrology and witchcraft fit together. One of the best ways to do this is to talk about it with other practitioners. Look for online discussions, and if there is a local metaphysical shop, check to see if they have classes or discussion groups. If you don't find what you need, consider creating a study group. Learning more about your own birth chart is also an excellent next step.

At some point, you may wish to call upon the services of an astrologer to give you a reading that is fine tuned to your chart. There are services that provide not just charts but full chart readings that are generated by software. These are a decent tool and more economical than a professional astrologer, but they lack the finesse and intuition that only a person can offer. Nonetheless, they can be a good starting point. If you do decide to hire an astrologer to do your chart, shop around to find someone attuned to your spiritual needs. You may decide to learn enough astrology to read your own chart, and that will serve you for many reasons. However, most practitioners of a divinatory art will seek out another practitioner rather than read for themselves in important matters. It is hard to see some things when you are too attached to the outcomes.

If you find your interest in astrology and its effect on a person's relationship to witchcraft has been stimulated by this book, you may wish to read the other books in this series. Additionally, if you have other witches you work with, you'll find that knowing more about how they approach their craft will make your collective efforts more productive. Understanding them better will also help reduce conflicts or misunderstandings. The ending of this book is really the beginning of an adventure. Go for it.

GEMINI CORRESPONDENCES

May 21/22–June 21/22

Symbol: ♊

Solar System: Mercury, Uranus

Season: Summer

Day: Wednesday

Time of Day: Late Morning

Runes: Dag, Ehwaz, Odal, Thorn, Tyr

Element: Air

Colors: Blue, Brown, Green, Orange, Pink, Red, Silver, Turquoise, Violet, White, Yellow

Energy: Yang

Chakras: Heart, Throat

Number: 2, 3, 6

Tarot: Lovers, Magician

Trees: Beech, Chestnut, Hawthorn, Hazel, Horse Chestnut, Laurel, Linden, Oak, Walnut

Herb and Garden: Bergamot, Clover, Dill, Fennel, Iris, Ivy, Lavender, Lily, Lily of the Valley, Marjoram, Mugwort, Peppermint, Snapdragon, Vervain, Yarrow

Miscellaneous Plants: Anise, Eyebright, Horehound, Mandrake, Wormwood

Gemstones and Minerals: Agate (Tree), Alexandrite, Aquamarine, Cat's Eye, Chrysocolla, Citrine, Emerald, Fluorite, Howlite, Jade, Jasper (Green), Lodestone, Moonstone, Moss Agate, Quartz (Clear), Sapphire, Serpentine, Tiger's Eye, Topaz, Tourmaline (Watermelon)

Metals: Mercury

From the Sea: Pearl

Goddesses: Artemis, Inanna, Seshat

Gods: Apollo, Dumuzi, Enki, Hermes, Janus, Krishna, Mercury, Odin, Thoth

Angel: Raphael

Animals: Cattle (Bull), Deer

Birds: Chicken (Rooster), Eagle, Parrot, Raven

Issues, Intentions, and Powers: Adaptability, Balance, Change, Cleverness, Communication, Community, Creativity, Emotions, Intelligence, Knowledge, The Mind (Alert), Money, Relationships, Truth

RESOURCES

Online

Astrodienst: Free birth charts and many resources.

- https://www.astro.com/horoscope

Astrolabe: Free birth chart and software resources.

- https://alabe.com

The Astrology Podcast: A weekly podcast hosted by professional astrologer Chris Brennan.

- https://theastrologypodcast.com

Magazine

The world's most recognized astrology magazine (available in print and digital formats).

- https://mountainastrologer.com

Books

- *Practical Astrology for Witches and Pagans* by Ivo Dominguez, Jr.
- *Parkers' Astrology: The Definitive Guide to Using Astrology in Every Aspect of Your Life* by Julia and Derek Parker

- *The Inner Sky: How to Make Wiser Choices for a More Fulfilling Life* by Steven Forrest
- *Predictive Astrology: Tools to Forecast Your Life and Create Your Brightest Future* by Bernadette Brady
- *Chart Interpretation Handbook: Guidelines for Understanding the Essentials of the Birth Chart* by Stephen Arroyo

We give thanks and appreciation to all our guest authors who contributed their own special Gemini energy to this project.

Christopher Allaun

Chris Allaun is cofounder and minister of The Fellowship of the Phoenix, a queer Neopagan tradition. He is also initiated in Traditional Witchcraft and the OTO. He specializes in witchcraft, spirit walking, necromancy, and energy healing. He has written several books on shamanism and witchcraft, including *A Guide of Spirits: A Pscychopomp's Manual for Transitioning the Dead to the Afterlife.*

Crystal Blanton

Crystal Blanton is a licensed clinical social worker. She is also an activist, writer, mother, wife, and priestess. Crystal works in mental health program management and runs a small private practice. She is the author of *Bridging the Gap* and *Pain and Faith in a Wiccan World.* She is the editor of the *Shades* of *Faith* and *Shades of Ritual* anthologies and coeditor of *Bringing Race to the Table: Exploring Racism in the Pagan Community*.

Irene Glasse

Irene Glasse is a mystic witch, minister, blogger, yoga teacher, musician (Kindred Crow), and former marine with a background in journalism. She is a longtime teacher of witchcraft, meditation, and magic in the mid-Atlantic. She is the coauthor of *Blackfeather Mystery School: The Magpie Training* (Dragon Alchemy Publishing, 2022).

Dawn Aurora Hunt

Dawn Aurora Hunt, owner of Cucina Aurora Kitchen Witchery, is the author of *A Kitchen Witch's Guide to Love & Romance* and *Kitchen Witchcraft for Beginners*. Though not born under the sign of Gemini, she combines knowledge of spiritual goals and magickal ingredients to create recipes for all Sun signs in this series. She is a Scorpio. Find her at www.CucinaAurora.com.

Sandra Kynes

Sandra Kynes (Midcoast Maine) is the author of seventeen books, including *Mixing Essential Oils for Magic*, *Magical Symbols and Alphabets*, *Crystal Magic*, *Plant Magic*, and *Sea Magic*. Excerpted content from her book *Llewellyn's Complete Book of Correspondences* has been used throughout this series, and she is a Scorpio. Find her at http://www.kynes.net.

Tiffany Lazic

Tiffany Lazic is a registered psychotherapist, spiritual director, certified Havening Techniques practitioner, and an ever-inquisitive Gemini newly transplanted from Canada to Wales. She is the author of *The Great Work: Self-Knowledge and Healing Through the Wheel of the Year* and *The Noble Art: From Shadow to Essence Through the Wheel of the Year*.

Najah Lightfoot

Najah Lightfoot is the multi-award-winning author of the bestselling *Good Juju: Mojos, Rites & Practices for the Magical Soul* and *Powerful Juju: Goddesses, Music & Magic for Comfort, Guidance & Protection*. She is a contributor to *The Library of Esoterica-Volume III, Witchcraft*, and can be found online @NajahLightfoot on Instagram and Facebook.

Austin Nix

Austin Nix is an occultist from Fayetteville, North Carolina, with a specific interest in astrology, Thelema, and mysticism. He initially became involved with the larger occult community by growing a following on TikTok during the first waves of the COVID-19 pandemic. He now hosts the *Millennial Magick* podcast where he discusses a breadth of topics concerning magick and spirituality.

Notes

Notes

Notes

To Write to the Author

If you wish to contact the author or would like more information about this book, please write to the author in care of Llewellyn Worldwide Ltd. and we will forward your request. Both the author and the publisher appreciate hearing from you and learning of your enjoyment of this book and how it has helped you. Llewellyn Worldwide Ltd. cannot guarantee that every letter written to the author can be answered, but all will be forwarded. Please write to:

Ivo Dominguez, Jr.
Laura Tempest Zakroff
℅ Llewellyn Worldwide
2143 Wooddale Drive
Woodbury, MN 55125-2989

Please enclose a self-addressed stamped envelope for reply, or $1.00 to cover costs. If outside the U.S.A., enclose an international postal reply coupon.

Many of Llewellyn's authors have websites with additional information and resources. For more information, please visit our website at:

www.llewellyn.com